UNSTOPPABLE

**Inspiring Stories of Perseverance, Triumph and
Joy from Trailblazing Women in Healthcare**

FAWN LOPEZ AND FRIENDS

This book is dedicated to all the remarkable women who are already shaping our world with their passion, strength, and unwavering determination, and to those who aspire to do even more.

Within these stories, remember that life is a journey, not a destination. With each step you take in your journey, know that you are part of a unique sisterhood united to uplift, inspire, and motivate you whenever you need it.

May these stories be your guiding light, fueling your ambitions and awakening your potential. If even one of you finds encouragement or a renewed sense of purpose within the pages of this book, our mission will be fulfilled. We simply ask that you share this book with others in your circle so that we may witness the transformative power of collective inspiration.

I am deeply honored to extend a special dedication to my beloved sister, Kim Anh Dang, and the late Ilana Klein, former Advertising Director of Modern Healthcare. Their remarkable actions truly embodied the spirit of this book. Their kindness, generosity, and unwavering commitment to making a difference have left an indelible impact on the lives of those around them.

PRAISE FOR UNSTOPPABLE

"UNSTOPPABLE is a book for everyone--women and men, people at the end of their careers or at the beginning, and people from any background or profession. The stories of resilience, risk taking, learning and failure, and love and caring for others are profound--all from amazing women who share the most challenging moments in their lives. Fawn Lopez has done a great service by sharing her own profound story and inviting a diverse group of highly accomplished women to share theirs. All readers will owe Fawn much gratitude for this special gift."

Nancy M. Schlichting
Former Chief Executive Officer,
Henry Ford Health System

"A timely book about life's lessons by successful leaders with REAL stories to tell and who never allowed their circumstance, however complicated, to limit their future potential. Their journeys demonstrate the joy that comes from the power of resilience and grit. A must-read for those who wish to be inspired."

Michael Dowling
President & Chief Executive Officer,
Northwell Health

"The amazing personal stories of struggles, hardships, resilience, gratitude, and hope found in UNSTOPPABLE provide both valuable lessons for women early in their health care journeys as well as thoughtful insights to reflect on for more seasoned leaders. Regardless of where you might be in your personal and professional journey, these powerful insights provide both inspiration to the reader as well as a reminder of the importance of being true to your values and what matters most in your lives. A wonderful read and opportunity to learn from an incredible collection of bold and unstoppable female leadership."

Carrie Owen Plietz, FACHE
President,
Kaiser Permanente Northern California

"Careers are constantly evolving that takes leaders from heights only imagined as early careerists to then confront the realities of life's highs and lows that are a combination of joy and pain. The stories tell us leadership's journey mandates bravery, expect the unexpected, honestly reflect on personal revelations about life's circumstances and grow to be better leaders for those whom we serve. The life of a leader is indeed a complex mosaic. Each "UNSTOPPABLE" can guide us to not only be aware of the challenges of leadership formation but also understand that we are not alone managing struggles as we pursue excellence."

Joseph Swedish
Former Chief Executive Officer,
Anthem

"I have had the privilege of knowing several of these women, both personally and professionally -their stories have served as inspiration to me over the years -but perhaps as important as their stories is watching them in action. They are natural leaders regardless of whether they are serving as a system CEO or volunteering in their respective communities. That is what a true leader is-their principles apply to all walks of life-not just while on the job. "

Marilyn Tavenner
Former Administrator,
Centers for Medicare & Medicaid Services (CMS)

"I read the inspiring stories of women leaders in UNSTOPPABLE *and marveled at the diverse backgrounds with common themes of important family mentors and role models (often a parent or grandparent) and the series of defining moments that helped them discover their talent and potential. Each of them shows grit and determination to supersede adversity – whether poverty, racial discrimination, abuse and violence, or bias as women and mothers about the options open to them. Each in their own way shines a light on the importance of creating their own path for their lives and finding ways to step over barriers placed in that pathway. Some found a straight career path and others took many twists and turns, but all have made major contributions as healthcare leaders, mentors, and role models for the next generation of women.*

Grateful I had an opportunity to read these personal stories and I am sure others will appreciate these insights."

Mary Pittman, DrPH
President and Chief Executive Officer,
PHI (Public Health Institute)

"Inspiration takes many forms. These are inspiring stories for anyone thinking of a career in the health professions – or working their way through the complexities of our time – about overcoming personal adversity and professional challenge. They are doubly inspiring, as many of the writers came of age and achieved what they did in a world where men had the advantage of tighter networks with bonds formed during training, through sports and in the workplace. However, these personal growth journeys transcend gender and provide lessons in courage and grit that offer insight and encouragement for all."

Jonathan B. Perlin, M.D., PhD, MSHA, MACP, FACMI
President and Chief Executive Officer,
The Joint Commission

It is with great honor and humility that I pen this introduction, reflecting on the extraordinary group of women whose stories have deeply touched my heart and soul. The diverse perspectives, backgrounds, ethnicities, experiences, and challenges present in this book serve as a testament to the multifaceted essence of sisterhood. Through their unfiltered stories of honesty and authenticity, these women have chosen to peel back the layers of societal expectations, revealing the true essence of their being.

As you read the pages within this book, I hope that you will be moved by the raw emotions, vulnerability, determination, unwavering courage, resilience, and joy demonstrated by these women. I also hope that you will be inspired to embrace your own authenticity and find solace in the shared human experience.

I wanted to express my deepest gratitude to my co-authors for entrusting me with their stories. Their willingness to open their hearts and souls is an act of bravery that has the potential to ignite a ripple effect of transformation. By telling their stories, they have become beacons of hope that guide others through their own journeys of self-discovery and empowerment.

-Fawn Lopez

CONTENTS

Fawn Lopez

Turning Points: My Journey Toward Retirement, Refreshment, and Renewal

As I look back at my life and career, I see a rippled strand of pivotal moments. In one moment, I realized that I no longer wanted to walk down my chosen path—whether it involved working 60 hours a week, waiting to take my dream vacation, or making the office my top priority.

I started to envision a different, more fulfilling future with new people, ideas, and opportunities. I launched a process of self-inquiry: What could I complete, learn, develop, start, or teach? And how could I consult, mentor, write, travel, explore, relax, and connect? What kind of new life was possible for me?

Life and work turning points are full of angst, confusion, and regret. But they're also marked by feelings of peace, joy, and anticipation of a brighter tomorrow.

In taking a turn and heading down a different path, I knew that I would come out better, stronger, and more resilient than ever before. I would take back the power to redirect the trajectory of my life and career.

Scattered emotions fell into place, and I discovered that I could move from chaos, anxiety, and confusion to calm, acceptance, and gratitude for a successful career and a blessed, well-lived life.

My Pivotal Moment

In 2022, I decided to retire after more than 21 years at Modern Healthcare. For 17 of those years, I served as the brand publisher and a corporate vice president of Crain Communications

After investing more than 40 years in the world of business, the blended vision of retirement, refreshment, and renewal emerged as a watershed moment in my life and career.

I was overwhelmed by emotion—from gratitude for my colleagues and success in the publishing business to melancholy and regret about the people and special moments I had bypassed or ignored.

I wanted to spend time with my husband, family, and friends. More than anything, I wanted to be there—fully present and engaged—when they needed a kind word, a soft touch, encouragement, hope, and guidance.

The significance of being fully present in a time of need was a tough lesson to learn. When my family immigrated from Vietnam to the U.S. in 1975, there were nine of us: my mother and father, six children, and my beloved grandfather.

My father was a colonel in the Vietnamese army. Before Saigon fell in 1975, he chose to risk his life and save his six children to seek freedom in America. Imagine the nine of us, crammed like sardines on the dark, cold floor of a cargo plane for a six-hour flight across the Pacific Ocean. We were frightened beyond belief.

And we were overwhelmed with questions. "Will we survive this rocky flight? Where is the U.S. military taking us? What will happen once we arrive? Who will help us?" None of us had the answers. But my father was determined to make his vision of a better life a reality for his family.

Our journey to America took us from Ho Chi Minh City to Guam to Camp Pendleton, a military camp based in San Diego. I still remember the night we arrived. It was freezing, and as the bus drove up to the camp, my mother and all the children started to cry.

All we could see was row upon row of military tents. I remember thinking, "Is this what we can look forward to? I thought we left Vietnam to find a better future in the U.S.!"

Eventually, we got our own tent—complete with nine cots. We stood in line for food and wore oversized army jackets the military had handed us to keep warm at night.

We eventually ended up in Kansas City, Missouri, a Midwestern city that would become my family's home for the next 48 years.

We arrived with a few hundred dollars and some food stamps in our pockets. But our hearts were filled with hope for a future grounded in freedom and the opportunity to pursue any venture we could imagine.

Life outside the regimentation of a miliary camp was difficult. There were nine of us. We had no money and no friends. And my father was the only one in our family who spoke English. Our challenge? To embrace a new culture and a radically different family dynamic.

Despite our status as refugees in a foreign land, we stayed hopeful and determined to build a life in our new country. But a routine trip to the grocery store turned into a painful reminder of our struggle. Devoid of empathy and sensitivity, a grocery store cashier humiliated my mother for purchasing seafood, a staple food in Vietnam, with food stamps.

My mother left the store in tears, vowing to never allow anyone to demean her or her family again. The very next day, both my mother and father began looking for work.

My father, the former army colonel, took on two jobs—one as a janitor and another as a steel worker—while my mother, born into wealth, took on employment as a seamstress at the age of 45. To ensure our family's survival, all six children also contributed by working diligently to generate additional income.

But my parents never let us see ourselves as victims. Their message was clear: Push through the toughest barriers and roadblocks, and don't let the sharp judgments of others shape your destiny.

My family was determined not to squander the opportunity we had risked our lives for. We embraced my father's vision of a better life and his pathway for getting there.

"The only way out of poverty is through education and hard work," he reminded us. "Money will come and go. But your education and integrity will be with you forever, giving you confidence to do things you might never have considered."

Those early experiences profoundly shaped the way I came to view my life, career, and relationships as they unfolded over the next half century. And they influenced how I would confront and respond to change.

I learned early on that change and transition are difficult and inevitable. I also learned that change is a positive life force, allowing us to surface new opportunities and develop skills like adaptability, resourcefulness, and flexibility.

My family's experience with my grandfather tested our ability to navigate change and move past tragedy. My grandfather was 72 when he came with us to America. He had spent his entire life in Vietnam, supported by a large, loving family. But he was never quite the same after arriving in the U.S. The man who was always surrounded by friends and buoyed by the laughter and joy of a large, ever-present family was alone for the first time in his life.

Each member of my family worked a full- or part-time job to make ends meet while he stayed home by himself. Worse, he found himself suddenly part of a strange community whose culture he didn't understand.

The isolation and lack of support gradually took its toll. In January 1976—eight months after we landed in the U.S.—my grandfather died by suicide.

The night before my grandfather's death, he and my mother had an argument about a dinner she had prepared. I could see the pain in his eyes as he left the room. I had planned to see him after I finished my homework but decided to postpone my visit until the following morning. Sadly, there would not be a second chance for me to offer him comfort, as morning never came for my grandfather.

The memory of finding my grandfather's lifeless body in the cold, dimly lit basement where he had been living still haunts me. And the unanswered questions surrounding his sudden death only deepen the sense of tragedy and loss that lingers to this day.

My grandfather's death sent shockwaves of grief and reflection through my family, leaving an indelible impact on my life and career. It was a pivotal moment that taught me the invaluable lesson of cherishing loved ones and seizing every opportunity to express how much they mean to me. After his death, I vowed to never again take a single moment with someone I love for granted.

Living in the moment became a new mantra for my life and career. I would reflect on the past but know when it was time to let go. I would look forward to the future without waiting for it to arrive. I would focus on the now, pay attention to small but significant gestures, give thanks, and surprise and delight those around me with random acts of kindness.

Decades later, I still reflect on the significance of my grandfather's death and how our society dismisses and marginalizes older people. Imbued with wisdom and experience, elders seek kindness and validation from every corner of society—from healthcare, technology, and business to entertainment, transportation, and housing.

> *Living in the moment became a new mantra for my life and career. I would reflect on the past but know when it was time to let go. I would look forward to the future without waiting for it to arrive. I would focus on the now, pay attention to small but significant gestures, give thanks, and surprise and delight those around me with random acts of kindness.*

In the end, my grandfather's passing taught me some of life's most important lessons. It made me more compassionate, empathetic, and mindful, and I will carry his memory with me always.

The loss of my grandfather pushed my mother into a deep depression. She was never the same again. She struggled to conceal her pain and guilt, burying her emotions deep within. But she remained steadfast in her commitment to create a better life for her husband and children.

My loving, selfless mother developed dementia after the passing of my second oldest sister. In 2016, my mother passed away at age

84, just 18 months after my sister's death. I believe she ultimately died of a broken heart.

My second older sister, Kim Anh, fell ill with glioblastoma in August 2014. She was smart, kind, loving, and generous. She worked hard all her life to save for retirement, but she died at age 58—just six months after her initial diagnosis.

We were sisters, best friends, and confidantes, even while Kim Anh lived in Memphis, and I lived in Chicago. Because of the demands of work, I was only able to see her on weekends during the last three months of her life.

Reflecting on her life-ending journey, I deeply regret not taking a month off to be by her side, cherishing moments, sharing stories, laughing, and creating new memories together. Sadly, there would be no second chances or do-overs.

And then Jesse, my husband of 24 years, was diagnosed with cancer right before Christmas in 2017. Chicago's Rush University System for Health took charge of his care, liberating me to feel confident and optimistic about his treatment.

Rushing between hospital, home, and work, I pushed myself to care for Jesse, avoid snafus at work, and fulfill my mission as head of the Modern Healthcare brand.

Looking back, I wonder if I could have been a better spouse had I prioritized family over career. But once again, there was no going back for a do-over.

Next, the crisis of cancer hit the offices of Modern Healthcare. Ilana Klein, who served as our advertising director for more than 20 years, was diagnosed with cancer in 2019.

Ilana was more than just an employee. She was a cherished partner and family member. Her essence manifested itself in boundless kindness, generosity, and a desire to always give more than she received.

Despite her illness, she remained a dedicated advertising director, never using her condition as an excuse to slack off. Her bravery and commitment inspired every member of the Modern Healthcare family. I feel blessed to have had the opportunity to offer Ilana my love, support, and gratitude for her friendship and remarkable life.

Although I can't turn back time and make things right with my grandfather, mother, sister, or Ilana, I can use the lessons I've learned from their life stories to elevate my present and future interactions and relationships with others.

Each of these events magnified the need to reprioritize work, family, community, and relationships to live the life I wanted.

I realized that I could no longer say "no" or "maybe later" to an invitation to spend time with people, provide advice, or share kind words of support. I could no longer make up for lost time or insist on second chances and do-overs.

I've learned that every decision comes with trade-offs: going on a business trip or spending time with a dying friend; developing a new proposal or comforting a colleague whose contract wasn't renewed; building an awards program or going to bat for a woman who's on her way to the C-suite.

The tradeoffs I made around career, family, friends, and community could no longer be accomplished in the same, casual way. I had to reflect on the short- and long-term consequences of each decision, scrutinizing what might be gained and lost.

For me, the lesson was clear and simple: In life and work, there are often no second chances. People rarely get an opportunity to fix or repair what they've paused or moved to the back-burner.

I decided that my new life—overflowing with refreshment and renewal—would be different. I would walk through a door into the sunlight and keep that door open for the women and men who came after me.

If I acted on my vision, I would move from a 60-hour work week and thousands of business decisions to a wide-open field of opportunity where I could invest in work, friends, family, private passions, and social causes.

I was excited and frightened at the same time, but I learned that I wasn't alone. Downshifting or backing off from a job, profession, or career follows a predictable emotional arc.

The choice to move on brings feelings of relief, elation, and hope. Next come fear, doubt, and disorientation, then a final transition toward stability and confidence in your decision.

I spent months moving through these stages, seeking feedback from friends and colleagues who helped me navigate my choices. The questions were relentless:

- Would I miss holding a high-level position in healthcare, America's most essential industry?
- Could I thrive without the comfort and support of my colleagues and contacts in media and healthcare?
- Could I sustain my identity and sense of self without the rigor of a full-time position?
- Could I keep my platform to nudge and change in areas close to my heart—from DEI, ESG, mental health, and health equity to women as leaders and the battle against racism, intolerance, and misinformation?

I answered "yes" to each of these questions, but not before I zeroed in on my re-engineered mission/purpose, vision, and values.

Purpose and mission: Who is Fawn Lopez—not just Fawn of the past and present, but Fawn of the future?

Vision/aspiration: Where am I headed as a person and professional? And what roadmap will guide the next steps of my life and career journey?

Values: What are the standards or criteria by which I will make choices in the years ahead? Will I anchor my future in perseverance, courage, integrity, and determination? Or will I build my life on a foundation of generosity, empathy, and altruism?

My parents instilled in me and my siblings the values of gratitude and appreciation for the kindness and generosity of people we met along the way and the opportunities they shared. But just as vital was giving back and paying it forward, my parents wanted us to apply the blessings of success to make a difference for communities, society, and people in need.

Political and social events made the process of self-inquiry more poignant and urgent. America experienced a string of life changing crises—from COVID-19 and the murder of George Floyd to political unrest and threats against minorities.

The surge of attacks against Asian Americans during the COVID-19 pandemic brought to light the long-standing history of violence and discrimination against Asians and Pacific Islanders in the United States.

As someone who's personally experienced race-based bias and discrimination, I remember the wounds my siblings and I tried to suppress over the years.

Despite past traumas and recurring discrimination, I was determined to find the strength to heal, move forward, and build a more fulfilling life for myself, my family, and my community.

As I contemplated the prospect of retiring and embarking on a new chapter, I found myself challenged by the pervasive stereotypes and cliches that society associates with aging.

Instead, I had to create a personal vision that extended beyond a simple to-do list to an exploration of impact and making a difference.

TIMING IS EVERYTHING—KNOWING WHEN TO SAY GOODBYE

As I've gotten older, I've come to realize that recovering time is impossible. The runway of life and work grows shorter as time is compressed. And in practical terms, no one who has the good fortune to grow older has as much time to reflect, plan, launch a venture, or redirect a career.

Words like "someday" (i.e., "Someday, I'll get a new job or go on vacation") come with doubt and few guarantees.

I've also come to realize that many senior leaders must work harder to justify their status, position, and contributions. Society's focus on hiring young talent with "fresh degrees" magnifies this challenge.

As leaders age, they can never be last to conclude they're no longer relevant to the market, industry, or organization, or valued as they were in the past.

I've learned the wisdom of knowing when it's time to close the book or chapter and prepare to write a new chapter—or even an entirely new book. After all, moving on in life creates an opening for a smart, decisive woman to take the reins and move forward.

When I left Modern Healthcare for my still evolving future, I knew I would create space for others to make a difference in media and healthcare. I had a responsibility to know when it was time to say goodbye and open the door of opportunity to others.

In doing so, I came to the realization that so many others have already experienced: The world doesn't begin and end with one's job or career, nor does it determine one's identity and worth as an individual.

Even if you decide to close one door, a new door will open with experiences you never could have imagined if you had decided to stay.

Few things are more important to me than opening new doors for women and people of color—from those who face early life and career decisions to those who can savor what they've accomplished and look forward to a re-engineered future.

MY LIFE TODAY

My life today is more relaxed, flexible, and rewarding. I still contribute to Modern Healthcare by spearheading conferences on ESG, women leaders in healthcare, and behavioral/mental health. I'm working and collaborating with my husband, Jesse, on his company. I'm also serving on a couple of private boards and a women leadership group.

The husband I thought I might lose to cancer following a diagnosis in 2017 has emerged as a best friend, confidant, and co-worker. It's a blessing and a privilege to be at his side during much of the workweek.

In the office he established for me in Chicago's River North neighborhood, Jesse and I work together as a team every day. Rain or shine, we start our mornings with a productive work session before I whip up a delicious (and healthy) lunch for us in the office kitchen.

After lunch, we take a brief walk to recharge, and then we continue working until the end of the day, when we walk home together and enjoy each other's company.

In the years ahead, if either of us should experience a life-altering event, I can take comfort in knowing that I made the most of every moment with Jesse and cherished our time together.

I'll also move forward on other fronts:

I'll Leverage and Expand My Platform: When I arrived at Modern Healthcare in 2001, the late Jean Chenoweth, a veteran leader of the 100 Top Hospitals program, posed a thought-provoking question: "As the leader of the preeminent healthcare media company, what plans do you have for utilizing your new position and platform to make a positive impact in healthcare and your community?"

That question resonated deeply with me throughout my tenure at Modern Healthcare.

As a woman, refugee, and minority, I've learned that I must constantly strive to gain knowledge, skills, and experience to earn the respect of others and create a lasting impact on healthcare, publishing, and social justice.

I'm proud to have made a difference. And I'm proud to renew my commitment to advocating for causes that are near to my heart, including diversity, equity, and inclusion, sustainability, access to quality healthcare, and the fight against misinformation.

I'll Fight for Health Equity and Equality of Opportunity: My refugee family was too poor to benefit from traditional middle-class healthcare and too proud to visit public health clinics and emergency departments. Over the years, we learned a basic truth: In America, wealth makes health. We often hear the phrase, "Money isn't everything," but try walking down the street with no cash and no debit or credit card. Try buying groceries. Try renting an apartment.

I've learned that good health is both a gift and a lifelong journey anchored in the choices of individuals, families, communities, and governments.

So, I pledge to never stop fighting for health equity and broader opportunities in education, employment, housing, safe neighborhoods, and business development.

I'll Continue to Embrace My Identity as an Innovator and Entrepreneur: I've derived inspiration from the enduring values instilled in me by my parents, specifically the power of dreaming big and a steadfast work ethic. I hope to inspire others to follow a similar path by encouraging them to think ambitiously, dream fearlessly, and envision great possibilities. However, I also recognize the significance of starting small and moving swiftly to achieve our goals.

No matter where I travel in my journey of refreshment and renewal, I hope to inspire others to build, create, design, and re-invigorate every corner of life: business, education, health, technology, science, and entertainment.

I'll Continue to Advocate for Collaboration Between Men and Women to Drive Social Change: We can't forget that few women live and work in isolation. Men are part of women's lives—both now and in the future—as colleagues, co-workers, spouses, friends, and associates.

They confront the same set of decisions—to go into debt to finish college, attend graduate school, travel, marry, have children, buy a home, change jobs, and build a career.

As women spearhead change within organizations, they can't afford to marginalize the men who are willing to join them in the quest to create a more equitable, innovative society. Together, men and women can make it happen.

I'll Support the Sisterhood of Women Executives and Women Climbing the Ladder of Success: I've come to appreciate the uniqueness and value of women as never before. They have so much to offer the world—from the friends, family members, and acquaintances who punctuate everyday life to the icons who illuminate business, entertainment, technology, politics, arts, science, education, and healthcare.

The words and phrases that describe women leaders say it all: intuitive, sensitive, vulnerable, empathetic, inclusive, assertive, and democratic.

Women cultivate their nurturing side, protect their boundaries, foster teams, demonstrate respect, learn for mastery, and punch back against bias and poor treatment.

As the only woman minority in hundreds of business meetings, I've learned that hidden bias, discrimination, and even racism rarely disappear by waving a magic wand and quoting well-intentioned policies.

I want to empower women and women of color to get the recognition and opportunities they deserve in their professional lives. I want to encourage them to embrace their potential and aspire to leadership roles with open hearts, eyes, and minds.

Whether a woman is finishing her MBA, considering a career change, or moving toward retirement, she has—or will have—what it takes to succeed as a leader.

The decision to retire, refresh, and renew my life and work is challenging but also liberating. Patterns of thinking that once seemed carved in stone expand as never before. Doors open to new people, places, opportunities, and experiences. Lessons taken from life's peak moments and miscalculations precipitate turning point decisions.

Having the chance to navigate this life-changing process and impart my knowledge and experience with the future generations of women and men fills me with deep gratitude.

Fawn Lopez

Fawn Lopez is Publisher Emeritus of **Modern Healthcare.** Prior to her retirement on January 1, 2023, Fawn was publisher of the industry's leading source of healthcare business and policy news, research, and information for healthcare executives since 2005.

Fawn dedicated her entire professional career to the publishing industry. Prior to joining Modern Healthcare, she held the position of National Sales Director for Crain's Chicago Business. Before joining Crain's Chicago Business, Fawn served as Advertising Director at the Kansas City Business Journal in Kansas City, Missouri.

Currently, Fawn actively serves as a board member of two privately held company, SourceOne Global Partners and Geocann, where her expertise and insights contribute to their strategic direction and decision-making processes. In addition, she holds a position on the Dean's Advisory Council for DePaul University-College of Communication. Fawn's dedication to professional networks is evident through her memberships in Women of Impact: Leaders in Health and Healthcare, and The Health Alliance. She is also a fellow of The Institute of Medicine of Chicago.

Fawn has a passion for fostering and driving diversity, equity, and inclusion, not only in her organization, but also throughout the healthcare industry. Moreover, she embraces her role as a champion and an advocate for advancing health equity for all.

https://www.linkedin.com/in/fawndlopez01

Ruth E. Williams-Brinkley

Mentoring and Developing the Next Generation of Leaders: What I Have Learned

Growing up in the rural, segregated town of Girard (Burke County), Georgia, my role models were primarily Black teachers, a trend that continued from primary school throughout high school. My grandfather, a farmer, was busy operating our family farm, while my grandmother served as a teacher. My grandmother was college educated—rare for a Black woman in her generation. She always valued and prioritized education for her children and grandchildren. My mother was also a teacher, and the trend of teachers continues in our family today. Most of my family members who are teachers teach in primary and middle school.

While teaching young children is an incredibly inspiring and honorable profession, and was and still is our "family business," I never believed that I would be an effective teacher of young children. For that reason, I chose early on to do something outside of the "family business." I had neither the passion, talent, nor patience to live up to the remarkable role models I experienced growing up. These women and men took the time to teach us reading, math, and science. They taught us to appreciate literature, to reach beyond what we thought we could achieve. They taught us to reach for excellence.

While I knew what I did *not* want to be, I had no idea what I DID want to be. I was excited to attend college, but I entered college without a career focus. That lack of direction caused me to lose time and take longer to complete my education—however, I persevered and ended up with a career that allowed me to use my talents to contribute to society and still find great personal and professional satisfaction.

My grandmother turned out to be my first and most important teacher, mentor, and role model. She was a very hard worker, owning and operating our family's farm after my grandfather passed away. My grandfather believed that as a teacher, my grandmother lacked business skills. After his passing, however, she quickly developed and applied her business skills, allowing her to successfully own and operate our 200-acre family farm for the remainder of her life. That farm remains in our family over one hundred years after my grandparents first acquired it. While I didn't realize it at the time, my grandmother was teaching me to value education while also instilling in me business skills that I would carry with me throughout my career as a healthcare leader.

My career in healthcare began in nursing. I became a nurse because my grandmother decided that nursing would be a worthy and dependable career choice. She obviously realized that while I was not drawn to teaching, I was drawn to taking care of people who were ill. She recognized something in me and steered me in the direction of my talents, giving me two of the greatest gifts of my life—a love for learning, and an education. My grandmother's guidance led me to a career that allowed me to grow and develop all the way from my first role as a clinical nurse to becoming a healthcare executive. Along the way, I learned both clinical and business skills, building on what I'd learned all those years ago on the farm.

Living on a farm requires long days of work to plant, manage, and harvest crops, plus feed and care for farm animals. Of course, it also included going to school with mostly perfect attendance—a priority set by my grandmother. We were not allowed to miss school, and we were expected to study, do our homework, make good grades and make the honor roll. My grandmother and the farm workers did most of the farm work while we were at school. We helped in the afternoons and evenings after school and on Saturdays, and we went to church on Sundays. There was never much time to be idle. That experience working on the family farm prepared me with an extraordinarily strong work ethic and an enduring commitment to do my best at whatever assignment I was given. I still carry those traits with me today.

In addition to demanding work, growing up on the family farm instilled in me one of the hallmarks of my career—my curiosity and openness to take advantage of opportunities across various healthcare sectors and various geographies. This open-minded attitude allowed me to try new areas of the healthcare industry and reach higher than I'd ever thought I could. When things did not go as planned with our crops or animals on the farm, we had to figure out how we would pivot and support ourselves until the next planting and harvesting season; there was no other safety net. That self-sufficiency allowed me to become resilient and to always do my best to figure out what must be done. I learned that a commitment to problem solving and finding a path forward always leads to an answer and a way to achieve desired outcomes.

DARING TO MOVE ON

My career has taken me from the clinical setting to nursing leadership to business consulting and executive leadership. At each step of my journey, I had people who recognized within me skills and talents that I, myself, did not always recognize. Those people connected me to new opportunities and encouraged me to pursue those opportunities. They made themselves available to discuss whether a new role represented the right move for my career, and they encouraged me to always give my absolute best to whatever role I had chosen. Even if I was unsure I could manage the responsibility or if I was nervous to leave the comforts of a familiar job for the unknown of something new, I never had trouble saying "yes." My farm life resiliency, when coupled with the invaluable guidance and counsel of my grandmother and other mentors and sponsors, guided me to the right path. Along that path, I was able to meet my performance commitments and fulfill my personal mission and my career aspirations.

My first job was as a nurse at a large Chicago teaching hospital. This job felt like my calling. I loved working with nurse and physician colleagues and other members of the team. The nurses were graduates of the hospital's school of nursing, and so was I. They were strong, confident, and knowledgeable, and as I watched them work to provide excellent care to patients and excel at their professional responsibilities, I saw the vision of what I wanted to become. Being in the post-anesthesia care unit (PACU) provided me the opportunity to work very closely with physicians and other nurses and care for post-surgical patients who often required complex, life-changing, even *life-altering* surgeries. Our responsibilities were to help them safely recover from their anesthetics, monitor their post-surgical and any other clinical conditions, and transition them to their remaining surgical recovery. I found early on that I enjoyed complex cases; they stretched me and caused me to learn a lot about taking care of patients who had undergone major surgeries and who often had multiple medical conditions unrelated to their surgeries.

Despite the immense satisfaction I felt as a nurse, I always wondered what else I could do and what further impact I could make. Fortunately, I found people in my life who dared me to dream bigger. Part of moving forward meant that I needed to return to school to gain my bachelor's and master's degrees. Even though I was a registered nurse (who graduated from a hospital diploma school of nursing), I knew that it would be difficult to move forward in my career without getting my formal degrees. That led me to return to school as a wife and mother of two children, while I continued to work full time. These were daunting responsibilities, but again, my farm experience had taught me how to successfully balance multiple responsibilities in pursuit of my goals.

I have held every position available to nurses. And with each new opportunity came new challenges and the ability to learn vital skills and gain experience. I only managed to secure those new roles and the increased responsibilities that came with them because I had people who believed in me, advocated for me, and encouraged me to do my best, excel in my career, and work at something that I truly loved. It was not always easy, but it was always exciting and fulfilling. As a young, first-time nurse manager in the PACU, there were days when I felt overwhelmed, almost to the point of tears. The volume of patients coming into the PACU after surgery often seemed to exceed the number of nurses needed to care for them. When that happened, we banded together as an even tighter team to provide safe, quality care for our patients. There were many days when I went home exhausted, a bit shaken, and yet deeply satisfied that we had successfully provided safe and excellent care to the patients who trusted us to meet their health needs.

That same process repeated at every juncture of my career. When I transitioned away from nursing leadership to become a healthcare consultant, I felt I was entering a world about which I knew very little. However, my clinical, leadership, and critical thinking skills provided me with a firm foundation for working with clients to improve their operations. While consulting did not end up being a long-term portion of my career, I used invaluable tools such as critical thinking, problem-solving, and change management to help my clients move forward and advance their organization's improvement goals.

Over time, I became the CEO of multiple healthcare organizations, and again it was thanks to the connections I had made that these opportunities presented themselves. Each new opportunity gave me a chance to test my limits. My potential grew and grew as I continued to stretch into new territories. With each move, I carried my strong work ethic, resiliency, and a passion to provide excellent care and service to all those I served—employees, patients, and the broader community.

The Importance of Humility

In many ways, professional success requires a healthy level of both confidence and humility, both used in the appropriate amounts. We each must be the CEO of our own careers. Being the CEO of our own careers means that we must believe that we have a purpose in life that only *we* can realize, and that we are willing to work hard to achieve that purpose. We don't leave it to chance; we don't leave it to others to do it for us. Others will help us; however, we must believe we can master and excel at jobs that we have never done before. We must trust that our potential is limitless and that it is our duty to society to realize it.

At the same time, humility is as important as confidence because, to realize our best selves, we must be willing to ask for—and accept—the help of others. After all, success is a team sport! While our potential might be limitless, we can only reach it if we have people who can lift us up. We can only achieve so much by ourselves. With support, there is no limit to what we can accomplish. Successful CEOs surround themselves with people who can help them advance the organization's mission or purpose. As the CEO of your own career, you must surround yourself with people who can help you achieve your life and career purpose—while always giving back to help others achieve their goals.

> "*Successful CEOs surround themselves with people who can help them advance the organization's mission or purpose. As the CEO of your own career, you must surround yourself with people who can help you achieve your life and career purpose—while always giving back to help others achieve their goals.*"

It is this balance of confidence and humility that allows us to surround ourselves with the people we need. We must ask for help. We need the confidence to believe that investing in ourselves is worth our time, and we must possess the humility to acknowledge that we need help.

A healthy level of humility has made it easier for me to preserve my confidence. Over-confidence (or even arrogance) eliminates the valuable contributions of others that can help us. Setbacks become magnified because they make us question who we thought we were and what we thought we could do. Embracing the support of others provides confidence to succeed. And, just as importantly, that same support provides the confidence to fail.

New strengths require failure as much as success. One of the best ways to learn is to do something wrong (i.e., fail). Failure allows us to learn, adapt our approach and try again next time. This is also how we discover who we are as professionals and where our unique strengths lie. As a nurse, manager, and executive leader, I learned to watch those I admired and learn from them while adapting what I learned to match my individual and unique capabilities.

For the most part, I have maintained that same general approach at every level I have reached. Even though the challenges have gotten more complex, I still follow the same process. Try. Adapt. Try again.

Setbacks are inevitable and must be used as opportunities to gain experience and grow. That mindset is important for building resilience. Despite knowing that I would inevitably face setbacks at some point, I have had my confidence shaken during various stages of my career. I have suffered from imposter syndrome and questioned my capability or readiness to perform effectively in certain jobs. I have faced obstacles because of my race, my gender, and sometimes in new settings because, as I've been told, "you're not from here." And yet, I have met and made many friends who are invaluable to me, and who I would have never met had I not lived in some of the places where I found myself while pursuing my career. I have lived and worked in every major section of the United States, and in a few areas in Canada. Because of my work and my career, I have met the most wonderful friends—people I cherish and who mean so very much to me.

In addition to taking on new roles and responsibilities, we need to have people around us who act as safety nets—people who will catch us and reassure us that an isolated failure does not define who we are or the trajectory of our careers. These people are usually mentors or sponsors. Family and friends are important. Mentors and sponsors are gifts. We need people in our lives who support us—people who will share our challenges and successes and help us learn to respond with grace when things don't go as planned. And we need faithful family and friends—people who love and support us as individuals, whether we have big or small careers or jobs. These people love and support us because of who we are and because we are special to them, and they are special to us.

When something in our professional or personal lives hits us hard, it is important to take time to step back, evaluate what happened and what we learned, talk to a trusted friend, and give ourselves grace. As women, especially women of color, we sometimes have a natural tendency to try to do too much to prove our worth. The truth is, our worth and our value come from within us—not from what other people might believe or say about us. Yes, we must stretch and reach to test our limits and get better. However, we must be careful not to try to do everything alone; we must enlist others to help.

THE VALUE OF GIVING BACK: MENTORSHIP AND SPONSORSHIP

Equally as important as finding mentors and sponsors is our obligation to give back by mentoring and sponsoring others.

I am passionate about working to uplift those who are underrepresented in our industry and who want to succeed. Equity, inclusion, and diversity are supported through mentorship and sponsorship. And equity, inclusion, and diversity begin with leadership. Our C-suites and boardrooms need to represent the communities we serve, the workforces we have, and the diverse workforces we are trying to build.

As a Black woman, I am in a strong position to help diversify our healthcare sector. I mentor and sponsor other women to help them navigate this difficult career path and move past challenges they may encounter. When I walk through a door, I make sure to keep it unlocked and open so others may follow my path and walk through it themselves.

I am enthusiastic about developing leaders, and I believe it is my responsibility to share what I have learned throughout my career. Mentoring is one of the gifts we give back in exchange for the privilege of leading. I often reflect on the things I would have done differently if I had more mentors or had other doors been open to me. I want to offer the gift of my experience to other aspiring leaders. Simply put, our colleagues and "pupils" need our help and support.

We are all incredibly busy with the many obligations and responsibilities that compete for our attention and our energy. In today's professional environment, leaders have numerous expectations both inside and outside the work setting. We serve on boards. We have speaking engagements. We are expected to write think pieces, publish articles, and write book chapters, like this one. All this is incredibly important, and it consumes a lot of our time. And on top of all that, it is also vital that we make time to focus on our own health and wellness.

Mentorship and sponsorship are too important to leave to other people. These tasks can be time-consuming, but they are also immensely rewarding and impactful experiences. I have mentored and sponsored many younger female and male leaders, and I have learned from each of them. Sometimes, opportunities come about in surprising ways.

People who serve as mentors and sponsors for the first time are often eager to do so repeatedly because it is fulfilling, energizing work. People who want to become mentors should approach the role with insight, commitment, and passion. As a mentor, you must have insight into yourself and be willing to be transparent. You must honestly share past successes, failures, lessons learned, and wisdom. A mentor should also be patient and willing to allow the mentee to discover how to find their own way, offering guidance when it is necessary or requested.

Being a sponsor is one of the most powerful things you can do to benefit future leaders, your legacy, your organization, and our society, and it has been one of my life's greatest privileges. I am so excited about executive promotions earned by mentees or those I sponsored because I personally advocated for and sponsored them. I took the time to call and tell them about the opportunity and then let the "searching" organization know how much I valued them and their contributions. The candidate must ultimately "close the deal," but they may not have even gotten to the table if I had not advocated for them. It took some of my time and some of my political capital to do that. These people were all worth it, and I am incredibly proud of what they have each accomplished.

One of the greatest sponsorship opportunities that came my way was when a colleague recommended me for an interim position where I had no direct experience. She had seen my work in other areas and had confidence that my skills were transferrable. Her support and advocacy led me to my first health system CEO role. I am forever grateful. This opportunity came at a time when very few people with nursing backgrounds were chosen for CEO roles. I would never have gotten that initial opportunity had this woman not sponsored, advocated and stood up for me. It is my duty and my responsibility to give back and help others, just as she helped me all those years ago.

Mentorship and sponsorship are effective as life-saving medicine—both for the individuals, who will benefit from the guidance, and for society, which will reap the rewards of having more people realize their full potential.

I have had both a wonderful career and life experiences. I have also experienced my share of heartache and disappointment. Through it all, I have learned to look for the joy, the humor, and the grace! That is what has carried me through.

I. Am. Filled. With. Gratitude!

Ruth E. Williams-Brinkley

Regional President, Mid-Atlantic States

Ruth E. Williams-Brinkley is president of Kaiser Foundation Health Plan of the Mid-Atlantic States, Inc. In this role, Williams-Brinkley oversees all of Kaiser Permanente's care delivery and health plan operations in Washington, D.C., and suburban Maryland, Baltimore, and Northern Virginia. The Mid-Atlantic States Region operates 36 medical office buildings and has 832,000 members.

Williams-Brinkley is a trained nurse and a veteran health care senior executive. She joined Kaiser Permanente in November 2017, serving as president of Kaiser Foundation Health Plan and Hospitals of the Northwest. She oversaw all of Kaiser Permanente's care delivery and health plan operations in Oregon and markets in Vancouver and Longview/Kelso, Washington.

Prior to that, she served as CEO of KentuckyOne Health, Kentucky's largest integrated health system, a division of CommonSpirit Health, one of the nation's largest nonprofit health systems.

Before joining KentuckyOne, Williams-Brinkley served as president and CEO of Carondelet Health Network in Tucson, Arizona, and as president and CEO of Memorial Healthcare System in Chattanooga, Tennessee.

Williams-Brinkley serves on the boards of Travere Therapeutics, Natera, Inc., DePaul University, George Mason University Foundation, University of Phoenix, Greater Washington Board of Trade, Northern Virginia Chamber of Commerce, United Way of the Greater Capital Region, and Connected DMV. She has been recognized by *Modern Healthcare* as one of the 100 Most Influential Leaders in Healthcare, one of the Top Women Leaders in Healthcare, one of the Top Diversity Leaders in Healthcare, and one of Beckers Healthcare's most admired CEOs in health care.

She holds Bachelor of Science and Master of Science degrees with a major in Nursing from De Paul University, and an honorary doctoral degree from Spaulding University in Louisville, Kentucky.

https://www.linkedin.com/in/ruthwilliamsbrinkley/

Sherrie Barch

Derailed: Courageous Conversations in Your Personal and Professional Life

S he walked through the door, locked eyes with me, and said, "Welcome to hell."

This slight woman, with kind eyes but a stern demeanor, went on to describe how my family's world was about to change. No more birthday parties. No more overnights. No more babysitters. No invites to friends' parties. If you send him outside to play in the neighborhood, he might die in the bushes. And you might as well homeschool because no school nurse will be able to keep up with the demands of keeping him safe.

Our first-grade son, Harrison, had just been diagnosed with type 1 diabetes.

My husband and I were instantly swallowed into a whirlwind of information—insulin, insulin ratios, carb-counting, and how to finger prick for blood tests before using mini needles for insulin injections. But "welcome to hell" left us stunned. My husband pursed his lips, got up, and left the room without a word. He chose flight (maybe because he wanted to fight her). I did what I do in the face of a challenge—got curious. Why would this woman, a trained nutritionist and dietician, behave in such a manner? Where was she coming from? I asked her exactly that, verbatim.

I found out that her daughter had type 1, and that she was completely unsupported by her family, friends, and even her daughter's school, which had no full-time school nurse. She lived in constant fear for her daughter's safety, as did others around her. Birthday parties and overnights were out of the question, as other parents were afraid of a medical emergency happening on their watch. Her daughter was completely excluded. "Welcome to hell" and the list of restrictions she'd given my husband and I about Harrison was *her* worldview based entirely on *her* own personal story—not ours. And we hoped it never would be.

After initiating this courageous conversation with her, getting to the root of her alarming words, and regaining my composure, I went and had another courageous conversation—this time with the hospital administration. I was sure this woman was skilled and trained in her job, but the fact was that she was compromised due to her personal circumstances. "Welcome to hell" was not something I wanted another family to experience. I wasn't unkind or intense or dramatic, but I was efficient in my communication. As a parent and partner to the hospital, I spoke in good faith. I needed them to do better because I needed them to help us manage this new, scary situation our family had been thrust into, and that is why I spoke up.

At that point, I learned from the hospital that this woman was a floater from the cardiovascular unit, unaccustomed to educating diabetics and their families. After two courageous conversations, I'd gained the reassurance that this situation would not be repeated with another vulnerable family. She would not be compromised again—she would stay in the cardiovascular unit where her talents fit, and she belonged.

This story unfolded 14 years ago and became an example of how the same curiosity and desire for knowledge that had served my education and career so well was also valuable at home. I instinctively continued to acquire knowledge for the new challenge we were set to face. With no family history of type 1 diabetes, I needed to learn fast—and well. I read books, attended carb-counting classes, and pored over materials from the Juvenile Diabetes Research Foundation (JDRF) and the American Diabetes Association.

Here are a few quick facts. 37 million people have diabetes in America, 95% of whom have type 2. Children with type 1 diabetes make up about 200,000 of all cases. On top of that, approximately 1.6 million people over the age of 20 live with this chronic disease. Type 1 diabetes is an incurable autoimmune disease, not a result of lifestyle or aging. People with type 1 are insulin dependent for life.

The insulin part came as the biggest shock to our family. My reality changed tremendously overnight. For instance, I was no longer able to travel for work as much as I once did. Right before Harrison's diagnosis, I had traveled several days every other week for a year straight, creating the products and game plan for heading up leadership development and team performance at the company where I serve as CEO.

The good news was we were having family dinners every night (to count carbs, of course) and slowly figuring out our new life together. By engaging in more courageous conversations, Harrison *did* get invited to birthday parties and played in the neighborhood (without dying in the bushes). But I was never far away, lurking in parking lots or watching him play in the yard from the kitchen window.

I also continued to stay curious and ask constant questions—with both the hospital staff and Harrison—about what it felt like to have type 1 diabetes. He told me that sometimes it felt "icky" when his blood sugar was too high. But he also said he thought we were doing a good job with this uninvited guest. It struck me how right he was. We were all partners in coping with this chronic disease and managing the fallout. The bustle managing it daily created a layer of constant noise over our household.

But then, one day, it was silenced when Harrison asked, "Mom, when am I gonna die from diabetes?" I understood. The word "die" is in its name, right? Well, I was able to correct his seven-year-old assumption, but I was careful not to downplay the journey ahead of us.

Around that same time, we decided to invest in an insulin pump for him. This medical device would be another challenge for our family, but we knew it would help keep his blood glucose levels in a healthy range by delivering insulin to his body continuously, which is harder to do with individual insulin injections. Our entire family also attended training for the pump, where we also learned more about the early signs and symptoms of high and low blood sugars.

This led our fifth-grade son, Michael, to self-diagnose himself a week later. Less than a year after Harrison's diagnosis, Michael walked in the door after school and announced, "Mom, Dad, I think

I have diabetes." His blood sugar was 444. (Normal is around 80 to 140!)

As I sat in the hospital room with Michael that evening, my husband still en route home from the hospital, my mother called me in a panic. The alarm on Harrison's insulin pump was going off, and she didn't know what to do. I was talking her down when the doctor walked into Michael's room, saw me on the phone, and tapped his watch with a meaningful look that said, "This is the time I carved out to talk to you."

It was yet another opportunity for a courageous conversation. I told my mother to hold on, put my hand on the phone mouthpiece, explained the conversation to the doctor, and asked him point blank, "What would you do? Hang up the phone or ask for a few minutes because I've got an insulin pump alarm going off and we need to find out why?" He said, "I'll come back." When he returned, I thanked him for the opportunity to have this important conversation and for the space to focus my energy and attention on his advice and direction. His whole demeanor shifted when he realized I was knowledgeable and accountable for my family's situation.

The lessons I applied in that personal situation correlate directly with lessons I learned while growing my companies. I've always been curious about client needs, had courageous conversations, stepped outside of my perspective and seen a different point of view, and helped my clients confront challenges in the war on talent—all of which created space for me to grow as a human and parent. When clients are going down the wrong path, you need courage to confront them, discuss their talent needs and goals, and create a new pathway to success. I drew on those career skills that day in the hospital room and in other similar situations where I was called upon to be a family leader, advocating for the health and well-being of my sons.

Meanwhile, with two type 1 diabetic sons, one insulin pump, and a slew of other equipment and regimens to manage, challenge became the norm. Knowledgeable and accountable, yes, but I was also a mom on a wild ride through many emotions. I'd gone from being scared by Harrison's diagnosis to being angry about it happening to grieving the loss of our normal family life. And then, just as I was finally leveling out with Harrison's diagnosis, I was thrust right back into anger and grief all over again.

My family helped tremendously, and I built a network of type 1 diabetes advocates who provided support—sometimes it took a band of insulin-toting women to make sure every kid was in range. One evening, I spotted a young woman injecting insulin at a business dinner. I cornered her (with the best non-stalker curiosity I could manage) and found out she was a recent college graduate with type 1 diabetes, looking for a job, and she happened to be—wait for it—a gourmet chef! Soon after, Melanie joined the band as our carb-counting nanny.

At work, I had some courageous conversations about my less-flexible and greatly diminished ability to travel. We responded by hiring more team members to strengthen our existing foundation. And we found additional means to add value for our clients and candidates, including writing, speaking, sponsorships for women and diverse executives, leadership development assessments, and more.

There's a book called *A Beautiful Constraint* by Adam Morgan and Mark Barden about how to turn limitations into opportunities, which sums up exactly what I experienced. I had no choice but to think differently, and I believe that in the end, the clients and team members I served benefitted. Sometimes, as a leader, you need to be creative in solving your challenges and get out of the way of your competent teams.

I worked hard to train and transfer enterprise knowledge to our talented teams, create a clear vision of what quality and winning look like, and remove barriers that got in the way of our success. I'm happy to report that our organization's revenue growth since the year of my sons' diagnoses has tripled. I'm also beyond thrilled to report that Harrison, who is now 21, diagnosed at seven, and Michael, who is 24, diagnosed at 11, are healthy and managing their diseases well. They're curious about new technologies, like the Dexcom glucose monitors they have automated through their smartphones. They constantly seek out new information and tools to manage their diabetes. Michael registered with his university's disability center his first year, and they hired him on the spot because of his self-advocacy and ability to have a direct, courageous conversation about his needs and challenges as a student managing type 1 diabetes. He worked at the center all four years, helping students achieve better academic results. Harrison is now employed at his university as a certified personal trainer, where he helps students learn to exercise safely. My husband and I are incredibly proud of both young men for their courage and ability to have clear conversations and advocate for themselves.

Reflecting on these "after" stories (with "before" being "welcome to hell"), one thing became clear to me: I've done the same work as a mom that I've done for so many years as a leader! Our family worked hard to train and transfer type 1 diabetes enterprise knowledge to our sons, created a clear vision of what quality and winning look like for our life with type 1 diabetes, and removed barriers that got in the way of our success.

The lessons I've learned in my career and our family's type 1 diabetes journey are the same. Whatever system you're leading in— be it a family system or an organizational system—these lessons hold true.

First, lead and nurture with curiosity. Lean into your opportunities to find knowledge. Seek knowledge until you gain clarity and understanding. Then, continue being curious while you look ahead to plan and build your next steps. These knowledge steps will help you be a better leader and enhance your ability to provide clarity for your team.

Second, as a leader, you *must* push yourself to engage in

courageous conversations. Don't avoid them—practice them. You can make change happen simply by having the courage to speak up. And when you do, ask questions, seek input, and candidly share insights and perspectives. Your vulnerability creates space for others to do the same.

> "*Push yourself to engage in courageous conversations. Don't avoid them—practice them. You can make change happen simply by having the courage to speak up.*"

Third, you can't avoid challenges, whether in your career or personal life. Challenges happen, and beautiful constraints will always coexist as new pathways for your journey. For me, the biggest challenge was moving through the anger I felt (sometimes overwhelmingly) about my family being afflicted with type 1 diabetes. Instead, I chose to be grateful for insulin. And sometimes, when we bring together all these hard lessons and make a little room for embracing our beautiful professional and personal constraints, magic happens.

I am the CEO and cofounder of multiple organizations that specialize in executive search and leadership development. Recently, at one of those companies, a very competent and curious team full of knowledgeable recruiters completed a search for the national CEO of the American Diabetes Association. The talented leader we placed is already making a difference, and I find peace in knowing that he is up to the challenge of helping people with diabetes live longer, healthier lives.

There are constant reminders in my life—like this team and what they were able to accomplish—that a leader is a leader, whether at home, in school, or at work. We are above all else connected by our humanity, and by applying these interchangeable competencies—curiosity, courageous conversations, and our ability to respond positively to challenges—we can lead with grace and authenticity in all that we do. Curiosity unlocks our appetite for knowledge and helps us make space not only for challenges but for others. Being willing to initiate and engage in courageous conversations is an important communication skill for the execution of successful outcomes, the transfer of knowledge, and problem-solving. And challenges are the "real life stuff" that inevitably happens and creates constraint. How we prepare ourselves to respond shapes our reality.

How can you find clarity amidst these challenges, especially when facing problems that, by nature, trigger an emotional response and take you out of the productive state of mind needed to make good decisions? What information do you need to manage your next steps?

I define that problem state—where challenges are either dealt with or avoided—as the Workaround Bucket. This is a dedicated space where external challenges (like having two children be diagnosed with type 1 diabetes in the same year while managing a career) and internal challenges (dealing with the resulting emotions) collide. Without deploying tools like curiosity and courageous conversations, it's easy to languish and get stuck in the Workaround Bucket, living within your problems, and rationalizing them rather than seeking to solve them. (My other two leadership buckets are Roles and Plans, but that's a conversation for another book.)

If you ever find yourself swimming (or drowning) in the Workaround Bucket, don't worry. There is a way out. Ideally, you won't allow others to drop you into it. "Welcome to hell" could have easily pushed me right into it if I had allowed it. I could have accepted that woman's statement at face value, jumped in, and started dog paddling for my life, bringing my whole family, life-vests and all, right into the bucket with me. But instead, I got curious. I thought, "Who are you? Why are you saying that to me?" Then I initiated a series of courageous conversations as a way of not blindly accepting the reality that others were creating for me. Be your own best advocate.

If you do find yourself bucket-bound, take a deep breath, give yourself some grace (no beating yourself up allowed), and look for opportunities to lean into information, resources, and mentors or advisors. Engage your curiosity and be brave enough to have courageous conversations. Armed with this knowledge and support, you can build a ladder and climb out of the Workaround bucket.

If you feel stuck, ask yourself, "Is there a solution here that I'm not seeing because I'm not asking the right questions?" Remember that even when challenges seem insurmountable, you are in control of your destiny. Find the beautiful constraints, reframe them as an opportunity, and look for ways to work better and smarter within them. And don't let outside perceptions or terrible advice drag you down.

On the first day of school in his senior year of high school, my son Harrison Barch stood up in front of his new teachers and advocated for himself. "I have type 1 diabetes," he said. "I got this, but sometimes I need help. I don't necessarily want to be called out in class, but if I'm having a low blood sugar moment and I tap a classmate on the shoulder, it means I need them to quietly get up and help me get to the nurse's office safely. I'm also going to store sugar in your classrooms, so if I get up and grab that, I'm cool, no need to worry." He then asked everyone if they were okay with him testing his blood sugar in class. When the "faint when he sees blood" PE teacher said no, Harrison agreed to test himself elsewhere.

My son's courageous conversation lasted less than 10 minutes, and the best part was that I got to watch it from the back of the room. It took everything I had to emerge from that room without bursting into tears (I made it to the car). I realized that my husband and I, Melanie, and the band of advocates we'd met along the way had successfully transferred essential knowledge and skills Harrison needed to survive. But most of all, I knew in that moment that he was going to be okay. In fact, he was going to be better than okay. He was going to take better care of himself than me.

The same holds true in leadership. I am blessed to work with team members who are much better than I am in technology or legal matters and/or possess deep marketplace knowledge. I watch with wonder and pride as they expertly introduce our services to clients and assess candidates, building off the knowledge that I (and others) transferred to them. As leaders and parents, we teach, transfer, and model. Then we get out of the way, trusting that what we have given was received, and watch the ripple effect continue.

That's what legacies are all about, right? Built not by what we achieve but through those we inspire to achieve.

Curiosity, courageous conversations, and confronting challenges are three of the most valuable knowledge assets you can transfer to your team—whether that means the team at work around the conference room table or the one at home around the dining room table.

Sherrie Barch

Chief Executive Officer
Furst Group, NuBrick Partners, and Salveson Stetson Group
The Companies of MPI

Sherrie Barch believes that legacy is built not by what we achieve but through those we inspire to achieve.

Sherrie is the CEO and cofounder of Furst Group, a national healthcare executive search firm and NuBrick Partners, a leadership development and consulting company. She is also the CEO of a national retained executive search firm she helped acquire, Salveson Stetson Group. Her companies serve healthcare organizations and Fortune 500 clients and consistently appear at the top of executive search firm lists by *Modern Healthcare* and *Forbes*.

Sherrie's vision in progressing talent and creating opportunities, especially for diverse and women executives, has spanned 35 years. As a solutions leader in the talent management space, Sherrie has helped boards and CEOs recruit, develop, and retain their leadership teams. Her expertise in executive search and leadership consulting has made her an in-demand partner for organizations across the world.

Her forward-thinking approach landed her a spot in leadership guru Seth Godin's eighth "altMBA" program. The intensive and exclusive program attracts executives from the likes of Google, Nike, Microsoft, and Coca-Cola.

A seasoned speaker and author on leadership and diversity, Sherrie also wrote the bestselling *Heaven's Bell* book series on grief. She is currently finishing her third title, a business fable for new college graduates about the future of work (and what they don't teach you in school).

Sherrie holds bachelor's and master's degrees in business communication. She serves on the board of a privately held global search firm and is a member of CHIEF, a membership network for senior executive women.

https://www.linkedin.com/in/sherriebarch
http://www.SherrieBarch.com
http://www.FurstGroup.com
http://www.NubrickPartners.com
http://www.SSGsearch.com

Carladenise Edwards

LETTING GO OF BEING LET GO: LIFE LESSONS LEARNED

As a 30-year professional, I have had many highs and lows in my career. The first 10 years were incredible, the middle 10 were not so great, and the last 10 have been fantastic. Even the best years had downsides, while the frustrating spots provided glimmers of hope. The only constant I've been able to control throughout it all is how I responded. And my hope is that by sharing a few of the unpleasant, intimate details of my career, I will inspire those stuck in the middle to continue mustering up strength and resilience so they can get to better days.

I once heard someone say that all ideas are great until you are in the middle. It is typically halfway through a road trip, a rollercoaster, or a ball game that you ask, "Whose idea was this?" Then you get to the end and say, "Oh my, that was great. When can we do it again?"

Losing a job is one of those less-than-great experiences that can happen at any point in one's career. Getting fired is miserable. It leaves you feeling isolated and alone. You become convinced you are the only person you know who has ever been let go, and you start to think that you are a bad person or a complete failure. And then, you worry. You worry about everything from paying bills to losing health insurance to the impact on your professional reputation.

Talking about "being let go," regardless of the reason, is quite taboo. It is one of those topics that we are socialized to never discuss. Just as we shouldn't discuss how much money we make or a woman's age or politics with strangers, we don't talk about getting fired.

But how are we supposed to learn and grow from the experience without an open dialogue? How do we demonstrate resilience and fortitude to our children and those observing our situation if no one knows what we are going through? We need to talk about it. We need to process it. When you lose your job, you need to work through it so you can get to the other side. It is too difficult emotionally to do it alone.

I never thought I'd be the person who would have to admit to being fired once, let alone four times. Can you believe that? I can't.

But, nevertheless, it's my reality. I have experienced the horror of being told, "Thank you, but your services are no longer needed" or that my position was being eliminated due to budget cuts four times in my life—and it stung every time.

So, without further ado, here's my story.

LEAVE THE EXCUSES AT THE DOOR

I was fired from my first job at the ripe age of 16. I was the birthday party hostess at the McDonald's on Mission Gorge Road in San Diego, California. A sophomore in high school, I needed a job to cover the cost of my hand-me-down car used to get me and my brother to school. Our neighborhood school didn't have transportation, and with both parents working, having a car or hitching rides was the only option. So, I needed to work to cover the additional cost to the family. I was so excited when I landed a job at McDonald's as a birthday party hostess. Back in the day, having a birthday party at McDonald's was something every kid dreamed of, and we believed only rich kids had the luxury of experiencing that. Suddenly, I was going to be in the position of bringing joy to such fortunate little people!

But before I could even host my first party, I was fired. Yep, fired.

It's a long, twisted story, but let's just say I think I could have stayed and salvaged my job had the manager not insulted my father, who had tried to defend my honor. In order to avoid a fist fight, I "resigned." It all boiled down to me not realizing when I accepted the job that I either had to check the grease board to see whether someone had scheduled a birthday party, or I had to sit at home and wait for my manager to call me on the phone. This was the '80s, after all—before internet, cell phones, answering machines, or caller ID. We only had two phones in our house, one in the kitchen and the other in my parents' bedroom, and if you weren't home, you missed the call.

When the McDonald's shift manager called one Friday night to say someone had scheduled a birthday party for Saturday morning, I was not home to answer the phone. On top of that, I forgot to go by the restaurant on my way home to check the grease board. I was in Tijuana that night, hanging with friends like every other high school kid in San Diego. Simply put, I forgot to check the schedule before going home.

When the phone rang the next morning and the manager asked me where I was, I immediately jumped up, got dressed, and had my father drive me to work. My father, who was livid with me for being so irresponsible, wanted to make sure that I apologized and made it clear this would never happen again. But when I got to the restaurant and explained that I didn't know there was a party, the manager became enraged and proceeded to fire me. My father stepped in and tried to defend me ... and then, well, the rest is history.

So what did I learn? (First, I thank God for whoever invented answering machines and, ultimately, cell phones.) Most importantly, I learned to own my mistakes, apologize, and leave excuses at the door. If I had started with an apology rather than an excuse, I think there may have been a different outcome. On the bright side, my father coming to my defense was further proof of how much he loved me. He taught me to always stand up for myself and not allow anyone to speak to me in a demeaning way—regardless of the circumstances.

PREGNANCY, PROFITS, AND POLITICS

The next incident doesn't count toward the official firings total, but let's just say it was a close call. I had an employer who learned I was pregnant and attempted to fire me as a result. This was early in my pregnancy, and I wasn't ready to share the news until I was further along given my history of miscarriages. However, my employer discovered my personal news when I accidentally left an ultrasound photo on my desk. I came back from my lunch break to find my employer holding the black and white photo and a notice of termination. The good news is that, with the assistance of an attorney, I was able to resolve the situation.

I eventually resigned from that organization. When I left, I promised myself that I would never again work for a company that prioritized profit over people. Sadly, though, I did not keep that promise to myself. (Well, I'm actually not sure whether my subsequent employers necessarily valued profits over people or politics over me. I'll let you be the judge of that.)

THE AUDACITY OF CONFIDENCE AND COURAGE

We now come to my second official notification. It was 2011, and my family and I had just completed our first year in the great state of California. We moved across the country so I could take on the role of president & CEO at one of the first, if not the first, public-private benefit corporations in the country. Why I thought little ole me, at the measly age of 40, was ready to step into what was known at the time as one of the most politically controversial roles in all America, I don't know.

The role required serving 22 board members from public, private, for-profit, and not-for-profit healthcare and technology companies, all with vastly competing interests. Some were deeply committed to maintaining the status quo. Many did not want the electronic health information superhighway we were tasked with creating to ever come to fruition. Others were strongly supportive of the exchange of health information—but only if they controlled who got what information and how or when information was shared. All 22 directors made it abundantly clear that my job was to serve the better interest of their respective organizations—meaning that my work should in no way interfere with their current business operations.

In addition to the dilemma of how to please 22 heads of multimillion dollar corporations with competing interests, I needed to build a team from scratch. The team and I were charged with successfully designing, developing, and implementing a technological, operational, and governance infrastructure for an electronic health information exchange (HIE). It would have to serve the most populous state in the country with a budget of $38 million, and it would have to be built in 36 months through a very public, consensus-driven process. Call me crazy, naive, incredibly optimistic, or just plain bold, but I believed deep down that, with the help of smart, dedicated people, we could pull this off—even if my predecessors had been so disenchanted by their own attempts that they refused to talk to me when I arrived on the scene.

In short, even after hitting all the milestones I was given as CEO and completing a solid roadmap for building a state HIE, I was politely told that my services were no longer needed. The board, it turned out, had decided to disband the organization and the effort. I resigned, and soon after the organization folded.

Some good came out of this process, though. California's failure to create the first electronic superhighway for the protected exchange of health information eventually sparked innovation and collaboration in the private sector like nothing America had ever seen before. The failure of the enterprise was a positive impetus for progress in what is now known as the digital health sector of our economy. And for this, I could not be prouder, even with the disappointment and feelings of personal failure that haunted me for years.

The hardest part was knowing that the company had been set up for necessary failure and that I was too naive to realize it. I had to admit that part of my failed leadership was the fact that I was perceived by others as overly confident, arrogant, and insincere, even if this perception did not match my intent.

I realize now that I lacked humility and failed to show the

right level of respect to my adversaries, who were *not* in favor of the statewide HIE. In hindsight, I also understand that this inaugural effort to build a public benefit corporation had to fail for the market to come up with a more viable and sustainable solution. These were very tough lessons, though invaluable to learn at a young age. And since then, they have helped me find success in many ways.

MAKING GOOD TROUBLE

In the case of firings No. 3 and 4, I'm not sure if it was the profit motive or politics to blame. But, as John Lewis would say, I clearly made some good trouble.

In both cases I was the second person to ever hold the position I held within the respective organizations. In both instances I was not fired in the traditional sense of the word—rather, the position was eliminated, and I decided not to stay with the organization. The newness of my role resulted in a lack of role clarity for both me and my peers, which led to their having challenges working with me and my predecessors. I also didn't make it easy for my peers to work with me given my unwillingness to conform to company culture, which was often rooted in doing things the way they had always been done. I was naive enough to believe that, when hired, part of my job was to disrupt the culture.

In both cases No. 3 and 4, my role became obsolete when priorities shifted from developing strategies for growth and transformation to a laser-focus on operational excellence and reducing expenses. I was hired to create something new—but then, due to the economic instability of the healthcare industry, maintaining and fixing the old became the focus of the organization. And so, my steadfast commitment to transformational change was no longer needed.

It hurts like hell when you are told your services are no longer needed. It hurts when you reflect on the vacations, family gatherings, and school performances with your kids you missed because of time spent at an organization that didn't value you. You regret those sleepless nights when deadlines and your job seemed more important than your health.

Why did I say yes to the fearless leaders who hired me to help them implement changes that were needed but not desired? Why did I think I had the fortitude to transform large, stagnant institutions or to even create a new one? Well, over time, I have come to realize that it is because my successes outnumbered my failures. And it's because I love challenges, hard work, and change. My father instilled a level of confidence in me that has served me well for the vast majority of my career.

In every role I held, I made a dent and changed things for the better. I have helped organizations create something new and sustainable, and I am confident *you* are capable of the same. It feels good when you have small wins at work. And when someone actually notices the difference you've made, it's like reaching spiritual nirvana.

In Reflecting on the Bad, Remember What You Did Well

The most important lesson I took away from these situations is not to focus on what I did wrong or could have done better. Instead, I choose to focus on what I *did right* and should do again. I see now that I kept getting fired because I'm someone who puts myself in the line of fire. I love taking risks. And I will continue to take on roles and enter spaces where I am asked to make foundational changes or solve seemingly insurmountable problems. I will last long enough to write the strategy, and potentially long enough to even start moving a few bricks. But my determination and unapologetic style may again put me at odds with an organizational culture that is not ready for the change I am tasked with creating. And if that's the case, off to my next adventure I'll go!

Getting fired can be lonely and sad. No one ever talks about it, and no one really wants to listen. But if you honestly reflect on your experience—what went wrong *and* what went right—you'll find your spirits lifted. Dust yourself off and proceed to your next opportunity to do meaningful work.

RECALIBRATE AND FOCUS ON THE POSITIVE

When you find yourself in that waiting period between roles, use the time to recalibrate and refocus on where you want to go in your career. Ask yourself: "What is my calling? What is my superpower?" Think outside the box in terms of how you define the success of your recent tenure. Reflect on the following questions during this period of rest from work:

> *Getting fired can be lonely and sad. No one ever talks about it, and no one really wants to listen. But if you honestly reflect on your experience— what went wrong and what went right— you'll find your spirits lifted. Dust yourself off and proceed to your next opportunity to do meaningful work.*

1. Did I maintain my integrity by doing my best without compromising my values?
2. Did the organization or the community benefit from the work I did while I was there?
3. How can I take what I learned and apply it, so I can do an even better job in my next role?

Learn to ignore and silence the negative talk in your head. Deep in your soul, you know that you are not a failure and that your higher power and the universe will provide for you. Focus on that truth. As human beings, we do what we can each day, and then we move on.

The energy we produce while we work is a part of the circle of life, and as long as we are producing positive energy, we are doing our part to make the world a better place.

For every difficult situation I have overcome, for every job that I was fired from, there have been an equal number of home runs. In addition to learning how to manage difficult people, navigate hazardous politics, and pick myself up after being gravely disappointed, I've learned what types of environments I thrive in and those that are not worth fighting for.

LET GO OF BEING LET GO

I now spend my time serving as a strategic advisor to CEOs and functioning as an independent board director. In this role, I coach and advise organizations on how to execute a thoughtful and deliberate approach to achieve their defined goals. I am in my comfort zone of creating new ideas and helping operational experts facilitate change without having to be in the difficult position of driving it.

I love this new space. I've learned how to make every good idea someone else's. I've learned how to create a healthy boundary between work, family, and play. I've learned how to listen more and talk less, ask more questions and give fewer answers. And most importantly, I've learned that I only want to work with and for people who value my intellect, experience, and contributions—people who respect me as a person, as opposed to needing me to be their token minority.

It may have taken 30 years and multiple firings, but I have now come around to the fact that I needed to let go of being let go to finally move on.

Carladenise Edwards

Dr. Carladenise Armbrister Edwards has 30 years of professional experience in the healthcare industry. She is an accomplished executive who most recently served as Executive Vice President, Chief Strategy Officer for Henry Ford Health, a $6.8B integrated healthcare delivery system headquartered in Detroit, Michigan. Prior to that, she was promoted to the position of Executive Vice President of Strategy for Providence St. Joseph Health, a $24B healthcare company headquartered in Seattle, Washington, where she also served as Senior Vice President of Contracting and Chief Administrative Officer for Population Health. Dr. Edwards has proven success achieving revenue growth exceeding $3.4B. Her academic background and professional experience in the fields of medical sociology, epidemiology, marketing and business development, health information technology, and healthcare financing make her a highly sought-after advisor, speaker, and director.

In 2022, she was recognized by *Modern Healthcare* and *Becker's* as one of the top Women Leaders in Healthcare. She was also named one of the 50 Women of Excellence by the Michigan Chronicle and elected President of the cohort by her peers. She serves on the board of Clover Health [NASDAQ: CLOV], CancerIQ, Mae., and Sound Physicians. She is also a strategic advisor to Parsley Health, Sami, Functional Fluidics and the Leonard Davis Institute of Health Economics. Dr. Edwards is most proud of her service to the community, including serving as a board member to Heluna Health, American Board of Internal Medicine *(ABIM)*, and Healthcare Financial Management Association *(HFMA)*.

Dr. Edwards received her BA and M.Ed. from University of Pennsylvania and her Ph.D. from the University of Florida. She currently devotes her time to community and corporate board service. When she is not working, you can find her reading and spending time with family.

https://www.linkedin.com/in/cdedwardsphd/

Sue MacInnes

CREATE YOUR OWN PATH

My mother gave me $10.00 in 1976 so I could start a bakery. I was 17 years old at the time and had just spent the summer in Stone Harbor, New Jersey, with my sister, Jenny, and my cousins from Maryland, Nancy, Willy, Scottie, and Heather. Nancy was my age and my best friend. Summers with my cousins meant lots of time at the beach, crème doughnuts every morning, sailing, crabbing, fishing, and boating.

Nana was Nancy's grandmother (her father's mother), and she would come to visit and tell stories of the Jersey Shore. One day that summer, Nana told me the story of Dana's Bakery in Ocean City, New Jersey. She said that Dana's would make cinnamon buns rolled so thin you had to unwind them to eat them. Crowds would come to the bakery and wrap around the block in line for cinnamon buns, cinnamon bread, and molasses cookies called Cry Babies. Nana said that when the owners retired, they'd written a cookbook, and she had bought it. The next time she visited, she came with that cookbook, which had been printed in 1966 and had a hard, cardboard front and back. The pages were typed and printed, and inside the front cover Nana had written, "To Suzie, from Nana MacIntyre, 8/20/76."

So, with the $10.00 my mother gave me, I bought flour, butter, yeast by the brick, sugar, eggs, and other ingredients to make cinnamon buns, loaves of bread, and Philadelphia butter cake (the bakery kind). I calculated what a cup of flour cost, an egg, a cup of butter, etc., and then I figured out the cost of a half dozen buns or a loaf of bread. I decided I would triple the cost and charge my customers that amount.

I walked around my neighborhood with my baskets and sold out in no time. When I got home, one neighbor called and asked for six dozen cinnamon buns—she wanted them ready in the morning to take to the nurses at her shift at the hospital!

Just like that, I was formally introduced to the business world. When I think of my authentic self and the chapters of my life, there is a clear, discernable theme. Each experience made me stronger, and the path had many twists—not linear at all. Somehow, there was a bridging of life, opportunity, failure, strength, creativity, and optimism. As a little girl under the age of five, I would design and sew outfits for my dolls. In school, I always worked hard and excelled. Essentially, I was what you'd call a type A achiever.

When I was 13 and going to girlscout camp, I decided I would go on a diet. Body image was a big deal then. My sister was tall and thin, whereas I was not-so-tall and chunky. Maybe today you would call my body normal, but when I got my camp physical, even though I had recently lost 10 pounds, the doctor said I was out of range for the current weight charts (I was only 110 lbs. and 5'5").

So, of course I had to take on that challenge. And because I was at the shore with my cousins for the summer, I had complete control of what I ate. I would eat an apple for breakfast, chicken broth and five oyster crackers for lunch, and whatever my aunt made for dinner—a small teaspoon of vegetables, a little piece of meat, and a noodle or two. I could make the meal last longer than anyone and was always last to finish. In a short time, I got down to 80 lbs., which did not go over too well with my dad. In fact, when he and my mother came down to the shore, he was visibly mad. But this was the same guy who'd told me I was fat growing up.

Around this time, my aunt read in the paper that there was a thing called anorexia nervosa. It usually occurred in overachievers who wanted to have control over something, and food was one thing they could control. So, between my dieting antics and my bakery business, when forced to pick a college major, I chose Dietetics and Nutrition Education.

That was by no means my dream career. My first choice was to be on Broadway. Throughout junior high and high school, I was always the leading role in musicals. I would scour the newspaper and find community theater auditions. I loved to be on stage, and I could act and sing in front of large groups of people without fear.

But good or bad, my dad said I needed to have a real job. And as a woman, I always needed to be self-sufficient and able to support myself. My friends went to New York City to acting school and Carnegie Melon for voice performance. And although I was voted best actress in my senior year of high school, I took the college path of Dietetics.

I see in hindsight how influential my dad was in my decision making. I had to go to a state school, and I had to know my major. None of my friends had to do that. So, my internal compromise was that I also minored in theater and music. And although I was not a major in the arts department, I probably did more performing than my friends who'd gone on to focus on theater. I even was the lead role in *A Little Night Music* in my senior year of college.

Here's the point of my story: Be authentic to yourself. All the skills I accumulated—baking, business and math, creativity, performing in front of others—became building blocks and foundational to what I accomplished next.

Here are a few more takeaways from my youth:

1. **My dad was influential. I was brought up to do what I was told.**
2. **My parents assumed I would be successful, so I never received recognition for my achievements.**
3. **I believed that my success would be my own doing and did not expect any special treatment. I felt that being female was just a thing and that if I performed well, the cream would rise to the top.**
4. **Setbacks made me work harder. I did not expect any handouts. Whatever was sent my way would be something I'd have to figure out and rise above.**
5. **I tried to make my parents proud. Their approval was something I always strived for.**

There were three different paths you could take to be a registered dietitian: a one-year dietetic internship, a master's degree in dietetics, or a three-year work study program. The dietetic internship was very competitive and the most prestigious route. At the time, there were 60 internships at various hospitals throughout the country. My requirements were that the position needed to be within a few-hour drive of my parents' home and pay a decent stipend. I was tired of being poor and working waitress jobs.

I applied to three internships and was accepted to all of them. I chose Perth Amboy because it paid the most and because when I'd gone for the interview, I'd loved the people and the curriculum. The day I graduated was the day I was free to move to the next chapter—both in my career and my relationships.

I've known my husband, Doug, my entire life. Our parents were good friends, and I even grew up calling his mom and dad Aunt Connie and Uncle Jack. Doug's grandfather would lead adventurous canoe trips in the Pine Barrens of New Jersey. We would pack up the canoes with camping gear and camp along the waterway. My sister and I were the only girls on the trips. Doug was one of five boys, and his cousins and friends were all boys, and the dads would go too. We would go on Easter canoe trips and fall canoe trips, trips down the Delaware and trips along the Delaware canal. When we got married, it looked like a planned wedding because we'd known each other our entire lives.

The week after I graduated from my internship at Perth Amboy, Doug and I got married and drove out to Denver, Colorado, where he worked and where I got my first big job at Presbyterian Denver Hospital. I worked as Director of Patient Services in the dietary department and loved it! I developed a program for diabetics that provided restaurant services for patients being admitted for diabetic programs. I worked non-stop, to the point where my boss even told me to "stop and smell the roses." I started at $15,000 a year, which to me was a lot of money! I was so grateful for a paycheck—it made me feel like, "Wow, these people love the job I'm doing!" They called me the crackerjack!

Somewhere along the way, I was looking at ads in the Denver paper and saw a job listed for an immediate move to Albuquerque. The job was looking for a dietitian to sell enteral feeding products from Ross Labs, and the role came with a company car. This seemed like a dream! I got the job, said goodbye to Presbyterian Denver Hospital, and Doug and I moved to Albuquerque, sight unseen.

My training from Ross Labs proved invaluable. I learned a vast amount about the digestive system, how enteral feedings were composed, and the effect of specific disease states. I was loving it … and in the back of my mind, I felt like the education path I'd taken in college was directly supporting my job and my career!

I say "Create Your Own Path" because I've learned that life or extenuating circumstances can and often do alter paths. So, you shouldn't put yourself in a box of "what you should do." Instead, you should embrace change and use it as a positive to bring new opportunities, expand your responsibilities, and venture into the unknown.

I was seven months pregnant when Doug met me for lunch and told me he wanted to move back east. Albuquerque is the dessert. It's brown, there's no ocean … it was the opposite of what we grew up with. He'd been given an opportunity with his company to move to Baltimore as a transfer (with expenses paid). I loved my job, was about to have a baby, had already lined up a sitter and loved my OBGYN. But to me, nothing was more important than keeping my family happy. So, we moved to Baltimore, and I was happy about it!

Two months later, my daughter Emily was born. I was searching for a job, figuring out how to put my life back together. Right away, I learned that women with six-month-old babies in 1984 were not very marketable. The assumption was that women like me would miss workdays, have sitter issues, and generally be an unproductive investment.

It is so strange how one job can provide skills in another job. After exhaustive interviewing, I finally landed a job with Medline. And as luck would have it, Medline was providing third-party Medicare billing for Part B, which included enteral feedings. I knew more about those products and what justified them than most, so I became the leading salesperson for that program.

However, having a third child and working as a commissions-dependent salesperson also led to a life of constant stress. Day after day, I was trying to figure out how to balance my work and home life. Finally, Doug volunteered to leave his job and stay home with the kids. He said that if it didn't work out, he would go back and get a job.

So, I was now the breadwinner and sole provider for our family. I was experiencing what the traditional "man" had to deal with in 1991, while Doug was dealing with a lot of judgement about why he was a househusband.

Our arrangement worked great, but the first year was a hard adjustment. I should have been happy that things at home were being managed well and that I could focus more time on my career. However, the pressure of a straight commission job and the stress involved made me think, "I can't do this forever!" It was a combination of the endless pressure of bringing in the money needed to support my family (money that fluctuated based on performance), being bored, and wanting to do something bigger. I approached my boss and told him I wanted to do more—I needed to expand and grow. The response was ... "OK, then you have to uproot your family and move to Chicago!"

Let's look at the facts at that time: I'm a woman and the breadwinner! (Wow!) The pressure was on *me* to succeed, and yet suddenly I'd gone to my boss and asked for *more*! I see so many women waiting to be asked to the dance, but that did not happen to me! I went out on a limb and said, "Why not me?"

And guess what? That was probably the biggest and best move

I ever made! By asking *myself* to the dance, I'd paved my way for even more success to come.

I started at the corporate office in Chicago as the Medicare specialist, then went on to be VP of Medicare, then started Medline's Patient Home Direct Program. I was able to create new programs based on market needs that were both successful and innovative. I had wings!

You could think of me as being gifted or lucky. But just like on those canoe trips years earlier, I was surrounded by mostly men in my new role. I had a couple of tough years, and I often cried or felt like quitting. But in those two difficult years, I proved to be a results-oriented leader.

And my efforts did not go unnoticed.

On a flight with the CEO in 1996 I said I deserved two things: the eagle award and equity in the company. At the time, only men received those things. But I asked, and I got it.

And then, a short while later, the president of the company took me to lunch one day and said, "We have a great running game, but we need a passing game. Would you run marketing for the company?"

So, to all my lady friends: Get over your fears! Don't be afraid to ask for what you want. If you do, you can produce great results, and you can bring other women up alongside you!

From the moment I decided I wanted more, I got more! And then, before my very eyes, my life changed! As Chief Marketing Officer, I made a list of goals and things I would do to change the trajectory of the company. Medline was exceptional at manufacturing and sourcing products and running an efficient family business, but I wanted to take the company to a new level and embrace the clinicians that used the products. I wanted to bundle exceptional products with educational support to provide greater value and differentiate Medline from other companies. I had no marketing background, so I studied on my own and read 50 marketing books. I observed how products were being used, studied government regulations, and memorized clinical guidelines from the CDC and the Centers for Medicare and Medicaid Services.

Great work comes when your mind is blank, and you allow solutions to enter it. Through personal experiences as a patient and a caregiver, I took a particular interest in designing Healthcare products. These types of experiences—coupled with a lot of self-study on relevant subject matter—formed the foundation that supported endless innovations. These innovations saved lives, enhanced our business, and changed healthcare. My mantra became: "We need to make it hard for the healthcare worker to do the wrong thing." In essence, we had to simplify healthcare for everyone involved, and Medline gave me the opportunity to do that.

Another life experience soon hit me and my family: the death of my partner. No one wants to go down that path. But when confronted, you have no choice but to deal with it and learn.

At the time, I was winning. But then, as it so often does, life reared its ugly head and interfered. I found out that my beautiful, fit, triathlete life partner, who has supported every career move I've ever made, had ALS . Being the fix-it lady, I was suddenly on steroids. I started to journal everything. My weeks leading up to the diagnosis were filled with travel, TV appearances, interviews, and customer meetings—all amazing career stuff. But then, in an instant, I realized that I had lost touch with life and reality. I look at those journals and think, "What was going on in your mind that work took priority over family?"

Doug was diagnosed on October 26, 2010. He knew the diagnosis two weeks before he told me. My travel schedule was insane, and he did not want to burden me.

For the next 19 months I tried to balance being an executive and caring for my husband and family. I thought, "What do I have to do now to make it great for him and for me in the future as a widow?"

Having an innate resilience, attraction to positivity, and inner strength helped me to manage the grief, figure out how to do the normal life things that Doug managed for me, and learn to be the rock for my children. Life is precious. Every day is a gift.

Through good and bad, each chapter molds us. Our decision is how we navigate through.

LIFE LESSONS

I'll end with this. Over the years, I have learned several vital lessons. Here are a few:

1. Leadership is professional and personal. Sometimes you need to experience the personal to understand how to be a professional.
2. I lived in a man's world. I don't regret it; in fact, it made me stronger. Maybe it is OK to say and understand that women work harder, have more challenges, and need to be challenged to live up to their potential.
3. Fear is OK! I was afraid of procrastination, especially when I had no idea how to do something (like run a conference, lead a focus group, or write a book). When that fear took hold, I ignored it—I read and learned about the subject matter until I was a pro, and then I did it. Failures will inevitably occur. But to me, failure was my best teacher. I would learn from my failure, then get it right the next time.

> *I lived in a man's world. I don't regret it; in fact, it made me stronger. Maybe it is OK to say and understand that women work harder, have more challenges, and need to be challenged to live up to their potential.*

4. The path to success was not about a major in college. It was simply about going to college, learning, and continuously challenging myself through personal, life, and work experiences.
5. Do what you don't think you can, and don't look back! That's the best advice I can give.
6. These days, my focus is on giving away as much as I know. I want to help others if they're willing to listen. Years down the road, will you do the same?

If I think about the core of my being—how I'm creative, driven, and resilient—I see that nothing's changed since I was five years old. It's been my experiences *coupled* with my core that has led me to success. Hard work and accepting that I needed to be more than exceptional to succeed … those were the tidbits and learnings I gathered.

Now it's your turn. YOU can Create Your Own Path!

Sue MacInnes

Chief Market Solutions Officer,
Medline Industries, LP

Sue MacInnes is an abstract thinker with the inherent ability to look at the "bigger picture" and understand the broader significance of information, ideas, and observations as they relate to improving healthcare.

As Medline's Chief Market Solutions Officer, Sue sets innovative strategy and cost-effective solutions to expand Medline's presence among the country's largest health and academic systems.

Sue has been with Medline since 1985 in pivotal sales and management positions. She oversaw operations and claims processing of Medline's Reimbursement division, spearheaded the Patient Specific Delivery HomeCare Program, and initiated a broad spectrum of clinical solution programs. Prior to her current position, Sue was the company's chief marketing officer for 10 years.

Sue's mantra is, "Making it hard for the healthcare worker to do the wrong thing." This thinking has led to multiple patents for urological, wound care, and patient-centered products that improve both clinical and financial outcomes.

Motivated by personal experiences and curiosity, Sue has an insatiable passion to problem solve and bring organizations together by redefining the rules of supplier and provider.

Sue graduated from Indiana University of Pennsylvania with a double major in dietetics and nutrition education. She resides in Trout Valley, Illinois.

https://www.linkedin.com/in/smacinnes/
https://www.facebook.com/sue.macinnes.5
https://www.instagram.com/macinnes248/

Stephanie Mercado

MY BIGGEST WAVE

I was on vacation with my family when I began writing this chapter. My boys spent a lot of the time at the beach learning how to surf. And in what must have been a meditative state, I connected this story I wanted to tell, to the experience of my boys navigating the waves. A metaphor emerged that brought tears to my eyes.

MEDITATION FROM THE SURF

If you stay in the sand, you never catch a wave. You will be safe, but also unfulfilled.

If you enter the water and turn your back to the wave, it will plow you over, pushing you forcefully onto the shore. If you head towards the wave but get scared and turn away at a critical moment, it will send you tumbling sideways, and you'll get rolled.

But if you get in the water and push straight towards the wave, keeping your face forward and your head up, you will reach the other side. And then comes the reward: the invigoration and refreshment of riding the wave back safely to shore.

I want to tell you a story about my waves and one tsunami.

BACKGROUND

The National Association for Healthcare Quality (NAHQ— pronounced Nay-Q) was founded in 1976 by seven people. These individuals came together with a common interest: to start an association that would make healthcare better, and to advance their own professional development though networking and learning.

As NAHQ grew, it did what most small associations do: contracted with an association management firm to handle operations. This included hosting NAHQ's member database, mailing due invoices, and administering the Certified Professional in Healthcare Quality (CPHQ) certification.

Over the years, NAHQ had grown its scope of work with the management firm to include five part-time employees and a part-time Executive Director, who interfaced with NAHQ's Board of Directors. In addition, NAHQ shared services through its management firm, which included IT, HR, Accounting, Marketing, and Customer Service.

While these administrative fees represented a cost-plus model, it was less expensive than NAHQ sustaining its own services, especially during this early stage of its maturity. Only larger associations can afford standalone status while sustaining operations and infrastructure.

By 2013, The healthcare environment and quality as a discipline had matured. The ACA act and many other environmental factors positioned quality as healthcare's leading strategy for the future.

It seemed like the sky was the limit for this small organization—but operationally and strategically, NAHQ was not prepared to take advantage of this opportunity.

The board rightfully believed that if the environment around NAHQ was changing faster than the organization was, the organization would be in trouble. The board made a decisive move to request their first full-time executive director—a leader who would help take NAHQ to the next level.

SAFELY ON THE SHORE

I received an email from a former colleague who was working at the management firm. It was June, and the firm had just posted the Executive Director role for NAHQ. Naturally, I thought I should apply.

I reviewed the job description and knew immediately: This was MY job. But there was one big issue—they wanted someone who could start in September. Not only did we have a three-year-old at home, but I was pregnant with our second child, due in September. So, a new job would be a no-go for me. I was disappointed but resolute in my decision. There was nothing more this pregnant woman could do but decline the interview.

But my friend was persistent. He encouraged me to apply anyway. He said, "If you're the right candidate, they'll wait for you." Wait for me? Good sign.

With that in mind, I began the search for clothes to wear to the interview. I wanted my outfit to scream "Executive director!" not "Seven-months pregnant lady." And when they called me back for interviews two and three, I went shopping again. For obvious reasons, this time around was much harder (outfit wise, I mean).

I did my requisite homework during the interview process, and the role became attractive to me for many reasons. I am a builder with heart and grit, and NAHQ was an organization that needed a turnaround. The job was to re-energize NAHQ's mission and build the business—two jobs that were in my wheelhouse. Second, the role was the perfect next step and compliment to my experiences. I had previously supported professional medical societies, so to move from supporting the "front of the house" of healthcare to the "back of the house" via quality leadership was a great opportunity to round out my experience. On top of that, the office was close to my home—a huge boon in terms of logistics with the kiddos.

I was offered the job in August of 2013, four weeks before our second son, Ben, was born.

Interviewing had already taken me offshore. Now that the opportunity was in hand, would I turn around and run back? No. Accepting the job represented my first wave with NAHQ.

Outsiders judged my decision harshly. First, they wondered how (and even why) I would do this with two little kids at home. They said, "Most executives are at a later stage in their career without the distraction of kids at home." Second, NAHQ was an important, but small and obscure, organization—even a past board member told me that the organization had peaked. And third, to others, it seemed like an unnecessary lateral career move.

Despite the naysayers, I remained confident in my choice. I could see what they couldn't: the opportunity to elevate NAHQ and Quality, overall.

So, I stepped down from my role at AAPM&R and took one week "off" before the baby was born. Then I took maternity leave for 12 weeks. Finally, on December 2, 2013, I returned to work as Executive Director of NAHQ and as the mother of two boys: Ben, 12 weeks, and Sam, three years old.

MY FIRST WAVE AT NAHQ

New on the scene, I assessed the opportunity for growth. I was energized by the potential, but also bewildered by the limited and shared resources of NAHQ and the management model.

I developed a mantra: *Start where you are with what you have, start where you are with what you have.* I chanted the mantra daily, sometimes hourly, as I worked with the staff and board to forge a path forward for the organization.

There were times I thought maybe I had hit a dud-wave, and that I should hop off and tumble back to shore. But I'm not one to give up; if we had not realized success yet, we were not done.

I worked with the small staff team and board of directors to begin the building process. We would grow the programs we had and build what did not exist.

NAHQ was the only organization that had staked claim on advancing the profession (and now workforce) in healthcare quality. Good news: We had no direct competition. Bad news: We

> *There were times I thought maybe I had hit a dud-wave, and that I should hop off and tumble back to shore. But I'm not one to give up; if we had not realized success yet, we were not done.*

had to invent and expand the view of the profession and convince more people to join us—*thousands* more.

Within 12 months we were exceeding capacity on webinar attendance, and I was being asked to make overnight decisions to increase our webinar investment by a factor of five, which would enable us to keep up with demand for engagement. At the same time, NAHQ was winning awards for developing the ground-breaking Healthcare Quality Competency Framework.

By 2017, Membership and CPHQs were up by 14%, and NAHQ was experiencing 10% year-over-year growth. Keep in mind, the average growth rate for any business (non-profit or for-profit) is only about 2-5% annually. But NAHQ, despite all the odds, was exceeding that metric—over and over again.

Of course, our success wasn't without its challenges. NAHQ was approaching the natural tipping point where it would be prudent to leave the safe, sandy shores provided by the management firm. Stand-alone status would mean more autonomy, more control over staffing decisions, and less sharing of resources geared towards the lowest common denominator.

I knew that a transition to stand-alone status was a huge undertaking. I'd heard war stories from colleagues who had done this before. The process generally takes about a year and is known among those who do it as one of the hardest challenges in a career. The amount of work, stress, risk, and heartache would be significant and at times overwhelming. Big risk for an undertow.

To delay this level of adversity, I began working with the firm's management on a solution. Instead of leaving, I wondered if maybe they could evolve with us and fill the voids that were becoming increasingly apparent. They tried their best, but the shared association management business model was simply not designed to accommodate the "big-box" client that NAHQ would become.

After consulting NAHQ's board of directors, we agreed that NAHQ transition's out of the management firm was imminent.

This was unwelcome news for the firm. Many stakeholders told me that a transition would be too hard, that the board would get scared and back down, and I would be left lurching and cleaning up the pieces. The emotional toll this took on me was significant. But I knew NAHQ would never reach its full potential if I backed down.

At the firm's request, I created three scenarios for an exit strategy.

> *Option 1: Enter in low tide* – Approximately three years to transition, peeling off services one-by-one until we were stand-alone. In effect, we'd be entering the water in low-tide, which would make for an easier ride.

> *Option 2: The five-footer* – Approximately 18-month transition, which would equate to a formidable wave, but totally manageable.

> *Option 3: The tsunami* – An eight-week transition that we'd have to attack head-on, without delay.

When the options were laid out, the management firm chose the tsunami, leaving NAHQ eight weeks to transition to stand-alone status.

I was shocked. I was overwhelmed. I was mad.

THE TSUNAMI IS COMING

I called the president of NAHQ's board, Nancy Curdy, to share the news. We discussed how to approach this, including the path of least resistance, where NAHQ would run back to the sandy shores of the management firm.

Nancy and I were aligned. NAHQ's mission was too important to stop now. Running back would mean NAHQ would fail to thrive.

We prepared to attack the problem head on, with gusto. No getting scared or turning back on this wave or the others that would follow.

When we left the management firm, we would go with nothing more than a list of our members and CPHQs, the money we had in the bank, and "the shirts on our backs." We had eight weeks to create *something* out of *nothing*.

We had no phones. No computers. No membership database. No way to process credit cards or checks. No bank. No way to add or renew CPHQs. No mailing address. No physical location in which to set up an office. No way to process payroll or benefits. No accounting software. No accountant. Nothing.

To protect NAHQ's customers and revenue from the force of the tsunami, we would have to build a "parallel NAHQ" and cut over to it without disruptions. The transition had to be seamless.

Nancy and I reached out to the board and shared the news. I told them, "This news will be hard to take. And your reaction may mirror mine. First you will feel overwhelmed, then you will feel mad. But you will only have a few minutes to process those feelings before I need you to move beyond them and get serious about solving this problem with me."

The board offered their unwavering support, and we prepared for the next chapter at NAHQ. Failure was not an option, and I was authorized unprecedented resources to set up the new NAHQ.

The risk was high for NAHQ—and for me. If I failed as a leader, NAHQ could quite literally cease to exist, and I would forever be known as the leader who led NAHQ into the tsunami it drowned in.

There was not a moment to waste.

First order of business was to talk with my team.

They were shocked. They were scared. But they believed in the mission, in me, and in our ability to thrive as a team.

The dialogue went like this.

Team: Where will we work?

Me: I'm not sure—let's find a real estate broker.

Team: How much money will we be paid and what kind of benefits will there be?

Me: You will have the same pay and benefits—but you're going to have to help me identify a benefits provider and a payroll company.

Team: Where will our operational infrastructure come from? What database are we going to use and how will we process credit cards?

Me: I need you to help source the vendors and set up the operations. We need to set up a world-class organization, better than the one we left.

FACE-FORWARD, HEAD-UP, GET ON TOP OF THE WAVE

I hired .orgSource to help with the transition. Their inspired and committed leadership was our life vest. The transition would not have been possible without Sherry Budziak, Kevin Ordonez, and Sharon Rice. They had the skills, experience, and the spirit to power through the tsunami with NAHQ.

We used quality tools like Work Breakdown Structures, Failure Mode Effect Analysis (FMEA), the Prioritization Matrix, and more. We were living with quality principles and leading with an incident command structure and culture. We were in "the zone."

This time around, our mantra was "No customer disruption, no revenue disruption." We lived by this, and all the decisions we had to make went through this filter.

Peter Gaido, NAHQ's attorney, offered great support as well. We spoke daily as we exited our contract with the management firm and entered into contracts with new vendors.

Picking our battles would be vital. I remember a moment where we were negotiating a contract with our would-be database vendor. The attorneys were negotiating key points, but it was taking too long. A days-long stand-off was simply not an option. If it could not be solved in minutes, we had to move on. Delays meant NAHQ would not meet the cut-over deadline.

The board, our staff, .orgSource, and our attorneys and vendors were all locked-in—face-forward, head-up, and prepared to get over the arm before the wave crested on us.

On the seventh day of the eighth week, we were in our new office, set-up and situated. Office. Phones. Computers. Payroll. Bank. Accounting software. And more.

I negotiated an additional eight weeks of IT support from the management firm, which offered us a little breathing room to transition the database and ecommerce function.

Still, 16 weeks was far short of the 52 weeks that is desirable for transitions of this type.

On February 1, 2018, the cut-over was complete. I invited the team into the conference room, pulled out my phone, and played *It's a Beautiful Day* by U2.

We did it. It was a rush and a relief.

BACK ON SHORE

Customers were not disrupted. Revenue was not disrupted. And we never dipped into reserves to fund the transition. We attacked the tsunami and maneuvered the wave safely to shore.

Since the transition to stand-alone status, NAHQ has improved upon its already impressive top-line revenue growth from 10% year-over-year to 16-25% year-over-year growth annually, which we use to expand our growing mission. Today we have more than 35 employees and about 10 contract-laborers outside of NAHQ. We have nearly 15,000 CPHQ and 10,000 NAHQ members. We've developed and validated the industry competency framework—again. We are advancing a profession, improving the workforce, and making healthcare better with quality. We have expanded our work to support healthcare organizations accelerate the impact of the quality in their organizations. Today, brands like the Veteran's Health Administration, Kaiser Permanente, and Christus Health are using the NAHQ framework and resources as a catalyst and strategy to advance quality via their workforce.

Successfully riding this tsunami and the mini-waves that preceded and followed it has put NAHQ at the top of its game. And I'm thriving personally too. We are award-winning and sought after as leaders in healthcare's quality and safety community.

At NAHQ, we've built a spirit and culture that is unmatched, and our lived experience tells us that even the most challenging situations can be overcome with the right work plan, the right attitudes, and quality tools. Even pandemics.

On a personal note, Life went on at home with my husband and the boys. I've continued to ride that transitional wave and all the waves that have come since.

The baby that I was mothering when I started working at NAHQ is now nine years old, and his brother Sam is 13. Like all working parents, I sometimes wonder if I'm giving them all they need. Am I a good enough mom? Is my time with them intentional? Am I modeling the behaviors I want them to express as kids and adults?

And then moments like this happen:

In the thick of NAHQ's tsunami in 2017, my oldest, who was in third grade at the time, unexpectedly ran over to me, hugged me, and said, "Mom, I love you." Having a very depleted "cup" at the time, I asked him to tell me why. I was craving more words of love and support. He resisted for a minute, not wanting to get too mushy with his mom. And then he said two words I'll never forget: "Stand-up."

When I asked him to define those words for me, he said, "Mom, I love you because no matter what, you do the right thing."

He was watching me struggle with that tsunami. He was watching me lead a team towards and over that wave—despite naysayers and multiple intentional efforts by others to have us fail. And he watched his mom succeed and make it back to shore. Only to ride more waves again …

The power of mother nature and the waves she creates serves as a powerful reference for me. And I am reminded that she still powers me today.

What's your wave?

Go get it.

Stephanie Mercado

CEO, National Association for Healthcare Quality (NAHQ)

Stephanie Mercado, CAE, CPHQ, is the chief executive officer/executive director of the National Association for Healthcare Quality® (NAHQ), the leader in industry-standard healthcare quality and safety competencies, training, and certification for individuals working in healthcare quality. Under Mercado's leadership, NAHQ has expanded its footprint to support healthcare organizations in developing capabilities and systematically building capacity for quality, leading to a more engaged and effective workforce.

Mercado brings more than 20 years of healthcare industry experience to her role. Since joining NAHQ in 2013, she has focused on understanding unmet needs to advance quality and safety and building solutions to solve these challenges. She commissioned innovations and introduced methodologies to research and define standardized competencies and develop never-before-available data and insights to drive workforce development. Confronting the challenges and creating a vision for the future has resulted in advancement of quality professionals and increased visibility and credibility of healthcare's quality workforce.

A highly sought-after speaker and author on healthcare quality workforce development and system sustainability, Mercado speaks nationally about strategies to drive healthcare quality and improve healthcare outcomes via the biggest lever healthcare has to affect change: the workforce. In 2023, *Modern Healthcare* recognized Mercado as one of the Top 25 Women Leaders, and she was awarded the 2023 Samuel B. Shapiro Award for Chief Staff Executive Achievement by the Association Forum.

https://www.linkedin.com/in/stephaniemercado-cae-cphq/
https://www.nahq.org

Ninfa M. Saunders

THE INTERSECTION BETWEEN WORK AND FAMILY: ARE THEY A CONVERGENT OR DIVERGENT PHENOMENON?

A CAREER AND LIFE TRAJECTORY ON THE MOVE

I n 1994, John R. O'Neil wrote *The Paradox of Success,* a book well acclaimed by business schools and the marketplace. O'Neil offered a different point of view and, in many ways, challenged the conventional wisdom of what it meant to win at work. With a newly minted top C-suite role as Chief Operating Officer of a health system, I was an avid follower of O'Neil's teachings, along with other well-acclaimed leadership authors whose focus was on the what, why, and how of professional pursuit and success.

My career trajectory could not have been better. Life at work and home was a beautiful storybook, constantly evolving to the next best space. My husband and I have two kids; at that time, our daughter was a freshman in college, while our son was in high school. Our kids were doing exceptionally well, and both went on to navigate adulthood in a manner that made us so proud.

In 2002, I accepted the position of Executive Vice President, eventually evolving into President, of a large multi-hospital health system in the Northeast. The role taught me well. I exponentially grew and matured as a top executive. Work, family, and life were in perfect synchrony. Both kids were pursuing their respective collegiate pursuits with purpose and alacrity. Work for both my husband and I could not have been better.

But then, in December 2011, everything changed.

THE EQUILIBRIUM THROWN OUT OF KILTER

The equilibrium of our life catapulted into chaos and despair on the evening of December 15, 2011. That day, our son arrived home from college for Christmas break. Like the dutiful mother I've always been, I started making all his favorite foods, a comforting feast of truly epic proportions. And like an equally dutiful son, he mindfully tasted everything and was most appreciative.

As fast as this anticipated homecoming came, his departure to meet his friends came equally as fast. After a quick hug and a kiss, he left on the fly to see them. As he drove off, he said, "Thanks, Mom. Love you, see you later." In the meantime, my husband and I were left with a table of food, wondering who would eat it all.

I decided to stay up and wait for our son to come home, intermittently dozing off as I waited. I knew he would be home before curfew (midnight), as he is the type to arrive home almost always 30 minutes early.

But by 12:30 a.m., he was still yet to arrive. And by 12:45, I had started to grow concerned. So, I woke my husband to tell him what was happening. He was more confident than I was, telling me not to worry and that our son would be home shortly. But by 12:50, I was in full-blown worry, frantically calling my son on his cell. I called and called, but to no avail.

Finally, at 1:03 am, our house phone rang. My heart sunk to the floor—I felt something was seriously wrong.

A police officer was on the line ... I can't recall entirely what was said, but it was along the lines of:

"Is this Mrs. Saunders?"

"Do you have a son named Jamie Saunders?"

"Do you live at _____?"

"Your son was in an accident and was taken to the trauma center. Please meet us there."

I did not become hysterical. But I do remember being stunned, petrified, unable to process, and utterly paralyzed. I could not even figure out where the hospital was and how to get there. My husband was in a similar state. I recall talking to the Director of the Emergency Medical Services for the health system I worked at, who volunteered to pick us up and take us to the hospital. It was the most prolonged and agonizing ride. I was partly perturbed during the ride listening to the EMS Director, who seemed to be incessantly talking about nothing.

Finally, when we arrived at the ER, he asked us to wait in the car so he could check on something. By now, my anxiety level was over the top, and my imagination was picturing the worst.

At long last, the EMS Director returned. What he said explained his most unusual behavior in the car. On that fateful night, there'd been two major accidents. Both vehicles had three passengers; in one, all the kids involved were killed. In the other, all three survived, but one kid was seriously injured.

Our son was in the latter of those accidents. He was the seriously injured one.

After what felt like forever, we finally had a chance to see him. Because the vehicle he'd been in would soon be engulfed in flames, they'd had to cut part of the car to pull him out quickly. I felt like sudden death came upon me when I saw our son. There were cuts everywhere and blood covering his face and toes. While he was conscious, he was not easily recognizable. They'd cut his clothes off, and I found myself alternately staring between my injured and broken son and the floor, where his bloodied and tattered clothes lay (clothes I remembered washing and ironing the last time he was home for school break).

The only thing I could do was cry, beg, and pray unceasingly for our son. I told him how much we love him and that everything would soon be okay. As I fixed my gaze upon our precious son, our baby boy, alarms from the monitor started sounding off fiercely. The curtain to the room flew open, and a team of doctors and nurses began frantically ministering over our son. I saw the monitor, and I knew things were bad. Everyone was frantically working on our son, including the code team. The only thing I could do was prostrate myself on the floor. I got on my knees and asked the Lord, "Lord, please do not take my son ... take me instead ... his life is unfolding ... please give him one more chance ..."

Eventually, the code team pushed me out of the room, even as I fought to stay. As I waved everyone off and tried to convince them

I was a nurse and needed to stay, a gentle presence wrapped an arm around me. She said, "Come, Dr. Saunders. Let me take you to the chapel where you can pray. I just asked my supervisor to give me the rest of shift off so I can sit with you." I do not know how long we were at the chapel, but dawn was breaking when the lead physician came to tell us that our son's condition was still critical, but that they had stabilized his heart and lungs and stopped the bleeding. My son was to remain in the ER trauma center for a little while before he was moved to the trauma ICU. He remained there for weeks until his prognosis improved.

Unfortunately, our son had broken several bones, from the clavicle to the leg, on his left side. He'd also fractured three parts of his spine and was placed in a body cast. His recovery was expected to be long, requiring months of physical and occupational therapy. The shock to the spine made it hard for him to stabilize his legs synchronously. And because of the body casts, he needed assistance in the basic activities of daily living. Spine fractures were a significant concern. His orthopedic and neurological team were cautious and could not say when he would be fit to return to school.

I knew that his recovery and rehabilitation would be long and intense. I knew I could not let anyone else care for our son. His care was something I was not going to delegate. He'd been given a chance at life, the very life I begged the Lord to grant him. As a result, I decided to leave a very coveted job to take care of our son. The promise of a career trajectory to the top paled in comparison to the promise of his life.

Much to his physicians' surprise, our son recovered swiftly, much earlier than expected, and was given clearance to return to school for the fall semester. He navigated life and school well despite some residual mobility and gait challenges. Today he is a competent young man and the father of our oldest and most precious grandson.

A Beautiful Tomorrow Emerges
Beyond the Darkness of Yesterday

As the nightmare and pain of yesterday becomes part of history, one's memory begins to amass and memorialize hopeful and joyful moments. A compendium of many moments of joy, hurt, desperation, challenge, faith, and hope becomes a catalyst for a new outlook, a chance for a renewed life to unfold, which brings with it a more soulful perspective and a strong resolve to focus primarily on what matters. In turn, this allows us to simplify life and let go of unwanted baggage.

Life takes many turns. We will never know what tomorrow might bring, so we must be steadfast and always remain hopeful that painful and tormented moments will become a foundation or a bridge for us to build upon tomorrow.

A Life Full of Blessings and
Gifts that Keeps Giving

Throughout my life—from growing up in the Philippines to spending almost all my adult life in the United States—I have been blessed beyond all knowing. At every moment and turn, someone or something enabled my path forward: a friend who lightened my load, a colleague who believed in me, a mentor or coach who helped frame my outlook, a teammate who inspired and held me up when I needed to be propped up, or a family that completes me and loves me unconditionally.

Perhaps you're wondering, who was that kind lady who held my hand and sat with me at the chapel during my breaking point? Well, she was an employee I had helped when she was on the verge of being wrongfully disciplined and terminated. She and many others stayed with me and cared for me during the lowest and darkest moment of my life.

As our son prepared to go back to school, I realized that I too had to return to work. I started my search for what and where my next role might be. There were several factors that were top of mind for me. First, I wanted to go back to the South and be home with my extended family. Second, I wanted to work alongside an organization where I could make a critical difference and bring with me the learnings of the past months. With deliberate pursuit and God's grace behind me, I was blessed to be appointed the first woman minority President and CEO of a multi-hospital health system in Georgia. A career trajectory once interrupted by tragedy now continues bringing with it gifts and opportunities that keep on giving.

REFLECTIONS

So, back to my titular question: Is the integration of work and family a convergent or divergent phenomenon? Let me say unequivocally that, judging from my own personal and professional experience, they are very much convergent. While some may have reason to believe they are divergent, it is crucial to consider one's individual point of view, life priorities, and the resolve they have adopted as they navigate work, family, and life.

In my mind, there are many thoughts and contemplations I've archived, and which now feed the soul. Therefore, it seems fitting to share them with you as nuggets of wisdom fortified by my life's work and my family journey. They include:

+ **The values you grow up with become the foundation that inspires and guides life's journey.** For me, these values were always about church, family, and community.
+ **One's professional life and work do not define the very essence of your person.** They are "identifiers" or "brands,"

describing and showcasing your talent and professional mastery.

+ **Personal mastery must be sharpened equally, if not more, than professional mastery.** We tend to spend more time nurturing our careers in a metered and well-planned manner, whereas personal mastery is often left to chance (unless you're faced with a personal crisis).

+ **People you meet and influence, thoughtful decisions you make about people, taking a moment to make a difference in someone's circumstance, acts of kindness to others, and mindfulness of what is around you ... all engage the heart and fortify the soul.** And they leave an indelible mark on you!

+ **"The Lord gave you but a small box to fill with your life's precious treasures. When filled to its maximum capacity, there will be nothing you can add to its finite content. If you ram things into it to fit, it will overflow, and its content will be irrevocably damaged. So, as you discern and gather life's ventures to fill the box,** be mindful of what you want to keep and treasure. Gather and keep only the most precious of things and the holiest moments." – *Fidel and Genara Medina, my loving parents.*

> *The Lord gave you but a small box to fill with your life's precious treasures. When filled to its maximum capacity, there will be nothing you can add to its finite content. If you ram things into it to fit, it will overflow, and its content will be irrevocably damaged. So, as you discern and gather life's ventures to fill the box, be mindful of what you want to keep and treasure. Gather and keep only the most precious of things and the holiest moments.*

♦ **We are writing the *book of our life* as opposed to a chapter in the book of our life.** The plot it holds is filled with ups and downs, joys and sorrows, light and darkness, triumph and defeat, and faith and hope. And the plot looks to a finale that only you can complete. So, endeavor to make it great, as you will be the author of the most meaningful, beautiful book of your life.

CONCLUSION

Is personal mastery and professional mastery a paradoxical phenomenon? Is the intersection between work and family and the journey to mastery a reality or a panacea?

Early on, I saw professional mastery as something that requires acceleration and exponential growth—sometimes at the peril of personal mastery. As a nurse executive at age 23, I saw an opportunity to forge ahead and make a name for myself. I made sure my qualifications were better than most. I had two master's degrees eight years after being appointed to my first executive job. I took on challenges that were not for the faint of heart. My work life was about building, creating, competing, and leading. Work was fun and addicting … the harder I worked, the more work I created.

Then life threw me an unpredictable turn—a situation I could not create, build, or lead my way through. When it came, it hit me like a ton of bricks, and there was no element I could manage or control.

What I learned from our son's frightful and crippling experience is a life lesson that has catapulted my orientation, resolve, and life to realize what truly matters: Our son is irreplaceable! There is only one him. Jobs will come and go, some better and more promising than others. But none could ever replace our son's life or the love and commitment we have and will always have for him. I begged the Lord for his life that frightful night on December 15, 2011, and He heard my plea and answered me!

The pursuit of success is, to a fault, a reality and not a panacea. But there is no bigger truth and reality than the pursuit of joy, peace, and love in one's personal life and family. Work and our professional accomplishments make up our brand and professional identity. But beyond that, still and always, family, the people we love, and personal pursuits define and complete us.

Ninfa M. Saunders

Dr. Ninfa M. Saunders has vast healthcare experience—from a bedside role as a clinical nurse specialist to various C-suite roles—and topped off her career as President and CEO of multi-hospital systems. As a healthcare executive, she maintained a laser focus on strategy, operations, and people while optimizing patient care and enhancing the bottom line. She created innovative strategies that accelerated growth, strengthened operations, and saved lives. As CEO of Navicent Health, Dr. Saunders expanded the hospital's reach in Georgia through mergers and acquisitions, partnerships, new service lines, and a strategic alliance with 30+ hospitals region-wide. In 2019, she orchestrated a merger with Charlotte-based Atrium Health to position Navicent for future growth and sustainability.

Dr. Saunders received her Bachelor of Science in Nursing from Concordia College, Philippines; a Master's in Nursing from Rutgers University; a Master's in Business Administration from Emory University; and a Doctorate of Health Administration from the Medical University of South Carolina. She also received her Six Sigma Black Belt Certification from the University of Michigan.

Ninfa is recently retired and sits on the Board of Directors for Horizon Blue Cross Blue Shield NJ, BioPorto of Copenhagen, Denmark, Quorum Health, T2 Biosystems, Medical Brain, and Wesleyan College.

https://www.linkedin.com/in/ninfa-m-saunders-7ba9941/

Teri Fontenot

GRIT AND GRATITUDE: HOW DISASTERS CAN BECOME BLESSINGS

A woman is like a tea bag; you can't tell how strong she is until she's in hot water.

–Eleanor Roosevelt

DEFINING MOMENT I

Bounding up my townhouse stairs late one night, my heart stopped when, in the dark, I saw the shadow of a person sitting on the inside landing. The intruder had a gun in his lap and a flask in his pocket. When he asked where I had been, I recognized the voice of my ex-husband.

Our tumultuous seven-year marriage had recently ended. We had dated for three years in high school and married a month after I graduated. Our beautiful daughter was born two years later, and I had been fulfilling my dream of being a stay-at-home mother with a plan to have two more children.

Then he decided that he had married too young, and he no longer wanted the responsibilities of fatherhood. Our first separation occurred before our daughter's second birthday.

He wasn't physically abusive then—just absent. He stayed out late while I was home with our daughter and worked intermittently. I vividly remember talking with a bill collector to avoid repossession of the car one evening while opening a pre-foreclosure notice on our house. He would leave for days at a time, refusing to tell me where he was going, with whom, and when or if he would return. Even though I told him my daughter and I would leave if his behavior continued, the threat did not keep our family intact.

It was shameful and heartbreaking. I'd been raised in a stable, nurturing, two-parent home in a small town, and I wanted the same for our daughter. I was popular and had an active social life in high school, yet he had convinced me I was worthless and that no one would ever be interested in me. I went back to him several times after he promised he had changed and that we would be a family.

He denied he was seeing someone, but evidence to the contrary was abundant—phone records, sightings of them together, anonymous threatening calls, and raw eggs thrown at my car. At 23, I accepted my destiny as a single mother. I also realized I needed a college degree to support my daughter. And I needed it fast.

While studying for an accounting degree, there were more separations, and then finally a divorce during my senior year. Upon graduating from college, I accepted a job in the city we both lived, hoping our daughter would have both parents in her life. He had little interest in either of us until I started dating.

The abuse shifted from abandonment, neglect, and emotional and psychological abuse to physical violence. He threatened one date, who filed a restraining order, and tried to run another off the road. When he hid in my home that night and proceeded to beat me (it wasn't the first time), I relocated near my parents in another state so they could help me raise my daughter. The final incident, again with a gun, occurred after I had moved. Luckily, a policeman saw him pulling me out of my car in a parking lot while our pre-school daughter watched from the back seat, intervened, and accompanied me to the state line. My ex continued to make threats even though he was 350 miles away.

My pulse quickens as I write this even though the events occurred over 40 years ago. And although it was the first real crisis in my life, it also represented salvation from a life of near poverty and lack of opportunity. If I had not earned a college degree and moved, I would not have had a career in healthcare. I also know that my experience made me more sympathetic to women in abusive situations, which was prophetic because my career followed a path to a leadership position in women's health.

DEFINING MOMENT II

A lumber and building supply company hired me as its controller; at the same time, I was taking MBA classes and preparing for the

CPA exam. An IBM salesman, Eddie, was attempting to sell a mainframe computer to my company and the local hospital. The hospital controller had resigned, and Eddie encouraged me to apply for the position. I had never thought about a career in healthcare administration—my knowledge of hospitals was limited to the birth of my daughter.

In 1982, a major event was occurring in Medicare reimbursement. Hospitals were being paid based on the cost of care, but rampant inflation made those increases unsustainable. The federal government shifted to a payment system that reimbursed providers for the average cost of treating a patient based on a specific diagnosis—diagnosis-related groups (DRGs). Suddenly, the risk shifted to the hospital to provide care within pre-established rates.

Sister Anne Marie Twohig, CEO of St. Francis Medical Center, sought a degreed accountant who could provide strategic financial support and oversee the accounting functions at the 450-bed Catholic hospital. She was a native of Ireland who had come to the United States with her order to build and run hospitals throughout Louisiana. She was also a registered nurse with an MBA. She could be tough and frugal—except when it came to the underprivileged and vulnerable patients we served.

I didn't know the difference between Medicare and Medicaid (government-funded health insurance for elderly, disabled, and low-income individuals), but at 28 years old, I dropped off my resume at St. Francis during a lunch break. Within a week I was invited to interview and offered the position. Sister Anne Marie was seeking a CPA for her executive team and was willing to teach me healthcare finance and administration. She was a pioneer for inclusion as made evident by the number of women and the gay member of her executive team.

During the five years we worked together, she expanded my role to lead non-accounting departments, attend medical staff and board meetings, and accompany her on trips to her order's U.S. headquarters. Sister Anne Marie was active in the American College of Healthcare

Executives (ACHE). She insisted that I become a member and encouraged me to become involved in nonprofit organization leadership and healthcare associations. As I represented her at local Chamber of Commerce meetings and state hospital association meetings, I was invigorated by opportunities to network and learn from other healthcare professionals. Sister Anne Marie did not define herself as a feminist, but she was acutely aware that there were gender inequities in America and worldwide. And as a female CEO of one of the largest hospitals in Louisiana, she embraced her ability to influence equality. I owe my career to her—she took a chance on a young, inexperienced woman and mentored me throughout my career and life.

I aspired to be a CEO like her. However, only nuns were hospital administrators in the three hospitals owned by the Franciscan Missionaries of Our Lady, and all other hospitals in Louisiana were led by men. I also thought that joining a company that ran healthcare as a business instead of a strong mission orientation would allow me to apply my MBA training. I had remarried, and my husband worked for a national company, so he was mobile. My older daughter was in middle school and we had a one-year-old daughter.

I accepted a position as regional CFO of a for-profit system in South Florida that owned several hospitals, assisted living centers, and outpatient clinics. Investments in related healthcare businesses were uncommon for hospitals, so this for-profit system was ahead of its time.

I was told I would be groomed for a CEO position. However, the system's financial situation was tenuous, and the corporate headquarters was run by executives who had not worked directly in a hospital. I was miserable because of the lack of quality compared to St. Francis and Sister Anne Marie's focus on patient care and mission. So, after one year, I left. A few months later, the system became one of the first acquisitions made by Columbia HCA.

Determined to return to Louisiana, I utilized my network and was offered a CFO position in a rural referral hospital that was half the size of my previous two hospital system experiences. It felt like a significant career step backward. The hospital was unprofitable, but I had the knowledge and experience to succeed, and we converted the money-losing hospital to profitability during my first year there. My role was expanded to include ancillary departments, and I enjoyed being back in a small town.

But my older daughter, who was entering high school, and my husband felt differently. My daughter's paternal grandmother had convinced her that she should live with her father. In addition, she and my second husband had developed a strained relationship. It was heartbreaking to think that I might lose my daughter, and I blamed myself. We went to therapy sessions, but she became unhappier. I was afraid she would make good on her threat to run away from home, so I agreed to let her live with her father. Promises were made that she would visit, write, and call, but when it came time for her first visit, she called the night before and said she wasn't coming. She added that I couldn't force her to come, and if I visited her, her father said he would hide her from me. Once again, I felt powerless and ashamed that my child was not with her mother.

Three years passed before she came for a visit. After she left, I found a letter on her bed confessing that she felt her father needed her more than I did, and that she felt sorry for him.

Defining Moment III

Fellow CFO Vicki Romero Briggs and I became colleagues through the Louisiana Hospital Financial Management Association (HFMA). HFMA had helped me significantly when I was at St. Francis with learning the basics of hospital finance. Vicki was a leader in our state chapter, had recently been promoted to CEO at Woman's Hospital, and was recruiting her replacement.

She approached me about the position. Woman's was an Ob/Gyn hospital and I was happy where I was. But my husband, who had lived in Baton Rouge before we met, was excited about the opportunity to return. The desire to become a CEO had faded, our daughter would be entering first grade, and I vowed not to move while she was in grade school because of the trauma that multiple relocations seemed to have caused my first daughter. Vicki was an engaging, smart, generous, and highly respected leader, and I accepted the position. The decision was pivotal, as it ultimately led to an offer to become president and CEO when she left—the role I ended my career in 23 years later. Vicki had an indelible impact on my life. We remain friends and now enjoy traveling abroad together.

Woman's had an incredible culture, outstanding quality and outcomes, and eventually became the only free-standing not-for-profit women's hospital in the nation. Services were expanded programmatically and geographically to position Woman's as THE women's health quaternary provider throughout Louisiana. It was also during this time that Woman's was called upon to fulfill its mission of improving the health of women and infants in the purest sense.

In the predawn hours of August 29, 2005, Hurricane Katrina made landfall, with its powerful eye crossing near New Orleans. It became the costliest and one of the deadliest hurricanes in U.S. history, destroying over 100 miles of the Louisiana, Mississippi, and Alabama gulf coastlines and killing nearly 1,400 people. Hundreds are reportedly still missing.

The storm blew through later that day, and at first the damage seemed minimal. But within 24 hours, levees that surrounded Lakes Pontchartrain and Borgne were breached. New Orleans, which is at sea level, flooded so quickly that the pumps either could not keep up with the water flow or they failed completely.

Residents who had not left the city took refuge on their rooftops if they could not swim or leave home by boat or vehicle. Hospitals and nursing homes flooded, and patients could not be evacuated due to the shortage of personnel, helicopters, and boats. Generators failed due to lack of fuel and water intrusion, and the August heat took a toll on the elderly and the sick. With no power, life-sustaining medical equipment could not be used. There was a lack of medicine and food, so treatment was limited. Toppled cell phone towers and an overwhelming number of calls jamming the ones still operable made communication unreliable.

Patients in system-owned hospitals were evacuated by their companies, but the largest hospitals in New Orleans were independent or owned by local governments and lacked the resources to rescue their patients. The Louisiana Office of Emergency Preparedness was overwhelmed and unprepared to evacuate hospitals while simultaneously providing rescues and shelter for hundreds of thousands of stranded New Orleanians at the Superdome.

When we learned that 121 critically ill and premature babies and several high-risk and postpartum mothers were locked down in five flooded hospitals, our team asked to take over the evacuation of the infants and mothers. We had some space, the network, a transport team, and special equipment to care for them. The state quickly agreed, and for the next three days, Woman's physicians and nurses coordinated the rescues with U.S. and Louisiana military personnel, who transported infants in Blackhawk helicopters. Wildlife and Fisheries officials from three states also rescued infants via boat and moved them to dry ground so that ambulances could transport them 80 miles to Baton Rouge. As patients were brought to us, we sent food, ice, clean scrubs, medical supplies, and toiletries back to the teams still in New Orleans.

The fates of the evacuated NICU patients and their families received worldwide coverage. Press conferences were held twice a day to find families who had scattered across several states. Many families didn't know that their infants had been relocated to Woman's, and it took our team nearly two weeks to reunite all of them. Our 82-bed NICU reached a peak census of 125 infants, and obstetric volume was 25% higher than average for nearly a year.

It was the most impactful singular event of my professional career… and the most gratifying. The crisis brought a unity of purpose and a unique opportunity to fulfill our mission in a crystal-clear way. Every transported baby survived. And Woman's was catapulted to the national stage.

DEFINING MOMENT IV

Before Katrina, the Woman's Board of Directors had challenged me to elevate the hospital's reputation by expanding our reach of quality services and outcomes. We had evolved from a "baby hospital" to a full-service women's hospital network that provided tertiary care, research, and medical education throughout Louisiana. Our vision was to share our expertise and knowledge so that all women, not just those in our service area, would benefit.

Around that time, I was appointed to the American Hospital Association (AHA) Maternal Child Council and served as the chair of the Louisiana Hospital Association. These roles exposed me to regional and national leaders. I was invited frequently to talk about women's health and, after our work in the Katrina rescue, leading in a crisis. The presentations and articles capturing these events put Woman's in the spotlight as a leader in women's health.

A colleague and AHA board member asked if he could nominate me as a trustee. I was honored, but I also thought I would never be selected because Woman's was an independently owned specialty hospital, and I was a woman from a southern state. But the AHA has long been interested in diversity, and that year their trustee skill matrix identified a need for executives from specialty hospitals, female CEOs, and representation from the South. I was elected, which was another pivotal moment in my career.

I worked with many influential leaders, learned governance best practices that were implemented with my board, and chaired committees and task forces. The three-year term went by quickly, and I assumed my AHA service was coming to an end. But at a meeting one day, Gary Mecklenburg, a former AHA chair, said, "Why aren't you running for chairmanship of the AHA board?" I was flattered that this industry leader would know me and stunned that he asked. There had been only four female chairs before me in the AHA's 110-year history—most of whom were nuns—and there had never been a chair from Louisiana. Gary offered to sponsor me, and I was elected in the first round.

Serving as chair of the AHA board provided the national stage Woman's was seeking. It also provided access to national political leaders, gave me access to the titans of our industry, and provided an opportunity to influence policy direction on the most pressing issues in the healthcare field. Working with the American Hospital Association was so rewarding that I aspired to become more involved in governance.

THE SECOND ACT

With my AHA leadership roles and appointment as the Audit Committee chair and director on the board of the Sixth District Federal Reserve Bank, my resume attracted the attention of board search firms. This resulted in invitations to join several publicly traded, private company and private equity sponsored boards. I also am serving on the Orlando Health system board. Upon my retirement and transition to CEO Emeritus in 2019, board service became my second career. I'm so grateful to remain engaged in strategy and be able to share my network to bring companies and providers together to strengthen healthcare quality and access.

To summarize what I've learned, these are the tenets I strive to live by:

1. Say yes when offered opportunities. Ask for them if they aren't.
2. Be authentic. No one else has the skills, personality, and experiences that make you uniquely you.

3. Focus on being better than you thought you could be. There is no need to compete with others, just with yourself. Do something every day that you didn't think was possible.

4. Be a mentor and seek mentors—they are the most powerful tools in a woman's toolbox.

5. Act like you belong in the room—be self-confident without being arrogant.

> *Focus on being better than you thought you could be. There is no need to compete with others, just with yourself. Do something every day that you didn't think was possible.*

In evaluating my life and career, an abusive marriage was the catalyst for change. The ingredients in the gumbo were determination, fear, luck, serendipity, and the undying support of my family, friends, and colleagues, who believed in me when I did not think I was worthy. I am forever indebted to them. Like most women juggling motherhood and a career, I worried that my family was sacrificed too many times. My fears were allayed when my younger daughter began her professional career. She had accompanied me to social events and keynote sessions at conferences and meetings while growing up and told me that she was so grateful for the opportunities to interact with influential and powerful people—a skill that most of her peers found intimidating but gave her poise and confidence.

My relationship with many of the women in this book began as colleagues; now they are my closest friends. I didn't know much about their pasts until I read their chapters but I noticed that, just like me, they did not use their struggles as a crutch. Instead, they used them as a ladder to overcome obstacles and emerge stronger than ever. We didn't know why we were drawn like magnets to each other, assuming at first it was because we were among the few women in healthcare C-suites. But there were other forces that caused us to gravitate to each other. I am blessed to have these women as confidants and trusted advisors. They continue to advise and support me and make me laugh, and I feel especially blessed to have relationships with them beyond our professional careers. I can't imagine taking my next steps without them by my side.

Teri Fontenot

Teri Fontenot is a high-impact strategist, visionary, and C-suite executive whose career has been in healthcare—an industry where disruption and risk are the norm. She is known for innovative thinking, leading beyond the status quo, working collaboratively, and leveraging her extensive industry network. She is passionate about adding shareholder value through effective governance and strategic direction.

Teri is an independent director on the boards of publicly traded and private companies as well as a not-for-profit health system with locations in the southern United States and Puerto Rico. She is also a strategic advisor to private equity funds and an SEC-qualified financial expert. Notable appointments include Audit Committee chair of AMN, LHC Group (NASDAQ), and the Sixth District Federal Reserve Bank of Atlanta. Teri has also chaired several boards, most notably the 2012 board of the American Hospital Association.

Teri's professional career included CFO roles in four health systems and president and CEO of Woman's Hospital for 23 years. She is the recipient of the Distinguished Service Award, the American Hospital Association's highest honor, and has been featured in _WomenInc._'s "Most Influential Corporate Board Directors" and _Modern Healthcare_'s "Top 25 Women in Healthcare" and "Top 100 Influential Leaders." Teri is an inductee of the Ole Miss Alumni Hall of Fame and LSU College of Business Hall of Distinction. She has two daughters, four grandchildren, and a pug, and her personal passion is animal welfare.

https://www.linkedin.com/in/teri-fontenot

Annette M. Walker

NO ONE HAS EVER DONE IT—
UNTIL THEY'VE DONE IT

 My daughter Jessi had recently taken a new job. She caught me for some work advice late one afternoon while I was preparing dinner. Somewhere between cutting the carrots and frying the chicken, she stopped me and said, "But, mom, I've never done this before!"

This comment gave me pause. I considered her comment, then responded. "Yes, that's true. But in reality, everyone, every boss, and every successful person you know has experienced the same situation. Don't let that stop you—**no one has ever done it until they've done it.**"

Then it struck me: The thing that worried her the most was precisely what attracts me!

Individuals like Joan of Arc, Amelia Earhart, and even Captain Kirk have always intrigued me because they boldly went where no woman/man had gone before. Not that the life of a healthcare executive is nearly as exciting as their adventures, but there are times when it can feel as treacherous!

Adventure—writing the script, forging the path—these are the kinds of opportunities I have found the most exciting over the years.

As most people enter their sixth decade, they think about toning down risk and adventure in favor of sailing smoothly into retirement. I must admit, I also was leaning in that direction, until the call came inviting me to a new adventure.

Perhaps you have been in this situation. Jessi's statement made me reflect on my reasons and focus on some learnings that I would like to share. It's my hope that no matter what phase of life you are in, when it is all said and done, this reflection will give you enough confidence and courage to take on new challenges.

I was hitting a great stride in my professional life and had just finished leading the development of a systemwide strategic plan for the third largest health system in America. It was a massive project, and I was thrown into the mindset of thinking about that middle space between *what is* and *what could be*. I was looking forward to a relatively safe and secure path that would eventually end in comfortable retirement. Without even knowing it, I was playing it safe.

Then, out of the blue, I received a call. "City of Hope is interested in you." I had known of City of Hope for most of my life. I knew it was an excellent cancer center and that it was in Duarte, but not much else aside from that. If you are unfamiliar with Southern California, we calculate travel in time, not miles—so on a good day, Duarte would be about two hours from my home. That was enough for me to say I wasn't interested.

But the response surprised me. "Wait—the job will not be in Duarte. We want to build a City of Hope in Orange County!" This new opportunity would be about 15 minutes from my home. While that would be great, I still was not sold on the idea. I had never worked for an academic or cancer center or planned anything from the ground up. I had never had any responsibility for construction or overseen a health system successfully enter a mature market with a $1B investment. I had an ample number of "nevers" to stop the conversation right then and there! Yet—something inside me kept the door open.

The opportunity was presented to me as little more than an idea—one generated because of a developer and City of Hope's CEO, who together had a vision to bring world class cancer care to Orange County. Land had been identified, preliminary thoughts sketched out, and there was a high-level overview of the community's need for advanced cancer care and research. These were just the kind of capabilities City of Hope was known for.

I started to contemplate the space between City of Hope' vision and reality. This is the innovator's path, one that I had always followed. The journey between the two.

Status, particularly hard-earned status, brings the security we all seek. I was working at a place where one of the ways leadership status was defined was the number of ceiling tiles in your office. Ceiling tiles defined your office and level of authority. My office at the time of the "call" had the highest number of ceiling tiles—144, to be precise—and was exceedingly generous with a 180-degree view and my own bathroom and conference room. Even more important than status, I had my people. My "go-to's." The relationships that take years to build and help you execute with confidence. The safe path, staying where I was, was the logical path. So why was the tension in this new opportunity keeping me up at night? That was the question I needed to answer.

What I learned was this: City of Hope had a rich history spanning more than 100 years. It had also opened many outpatient clinics; however, Orange County would be its first foray into exporting its academic presence beyond its original site in Duarte. While there was certainly much intellectual capital and expertise that would be supporting the effort, this ground-up development would be viewed as a complementary campus standing as an entity alongside Duarte. This would be a new experience for the whole organization as well as whoever would build the O.C. team.

Despite the richness of the legacy, O.C. would in many ways be a start-up. I had to ask myself, "Am I willing to risk the comfort, external recognition, internal influence, and all the perks and safety of my current infrastructure?" Forget ceiling tiles—I wouldn't even have a ceiling! I would not have walls! Just a big, shared space, a small staff, a Costco folding desk, and a cell phone. On the surface, it sounded like a bad trade.

I had to really evaluate if what I would gain would be enough for what I would be risking.

I got to mapping out all the pluses and minuses on a piece of paper. Starting something new would provide freedom from the usual baggage that comes when you inherit structures, buildings, roles, and other elements of bureaucracy of established efforts. In its place would come space for a vision, a dream, a chance to tend to something great and wonderous. It would allow me to test my skills, nurture my desire to lead, and make a difference. It would be a chance to build HOPE for everyone involved.

Hope is a word that is used in many ways ... but how do we hold it? Is it passive? Something you do without change? Entirely up to fate? I once learned that the Kanji, the two Chinese symbols for hope, mean two things: 1. A wish, and 2. Set far away. The Kanji and the Wish Set Far Away. Could I have both?

The thrill of adventure was calling me, but I was still torn. So, what was the tipping point? Well, it was older and more personal than you might think.

Around 100 years ago, a young mother in the northern parts of Minnesota realized that her child, my father, had a deadly disease, one that at its worst would kill him, and at the very least was likely to cripple him. No, it wasn't cancer—it was polio. This diagnosis sent a cold stone of fear right into my grandmother's heart—that same cold stone our patients feel when they're told, "You have cancer."

My family was far from the necessary medical services offered in Minneapolis. To give my father a chance, my grandparents had to make the difficult decision to travel almost 200 miles, over dirt roads and through snow, to entrust my father to the staff at Gillette Children's Hospital.

Imagine what that drive home must have been like, and then the many long months that came after, filled with sleepless nights wondering and worrying. There were no cell phones—in fact, there were no phones, period. Like many cancer patients today, my family could do nothing but wait.

This opportunity called to mind my father and my grandmother, but the faces I saw were my family, friends, and neighbors here in O.C. In the end, it wasn't risking the security perks or comfortable situation, it was that I knew in my heart I would make a bigger difference to the people I loved by saying yes. So, I did say yes. And I walked into the unknown.

Living in Orange County for 40 years had provided me with extensive knowledge of the community and the healthcare landscape.

I knew that to get out the gate I needed people who had the same familiarity and the right skills. So, I went for the best I knew, and they too grabbed onto the wish and the dream to build hope.

The first team of City of Hope O.C. consisted of myself, two executives, and one executive assistant—and we got to work! We were thousands less than my last job, but we were capable. I was grateful that these individuals had enough courage and trust to join me on this adventure.

Can I just pause to again mention I (we) HAD NEVER DONE THIS BEFORE! None of it. But I did know how to build the right team, inspire people, and trust at the right time. And I knew how to articulate a compelling vision that would enlist support both inside and outside the organization, which was our next step.

Our brand studies indicated that most of Orange County had a limited and incorrect knowledge of City of Hope, its capabilities, and how to access its services. We had no assets on the ground to deliver the services. It would take us 18 months to open our first office, in which time we still had to purchase land, plan, and build the campus. This was a unique circumstance and a challenge to create awareness, knowledge, anticipation, and ultimately demand—all at once. It was a delicate balance to not overpromise and disappoint. In those four years we rarely turned down an opportunity to share our vision, get involved in the community, and kiss babies. Oftentimes, we felt like we were running for office!

Our vision was to build a second campus in Irvine that included an outpatient cancer center and specialty cancer hospital, which we would complement with a network of care sites distributed throughout the county. Over the next four years, four people could not possibly do all that needed to be done. In coordinating with the clinical and technical experts in Duarte, we set about planning the needs of the cancer center and hospital. By year two, we had grown to a core team of 15. While that seems small, this is where the startup mentality became increasingly important. Everyone we chose knew we would be operating in a very informal environment where job descriptions were loose, and everyone just did what needed to be done.

If you are to be successful, you must be comfortable with change and ambiguity. These are not attributes generally nurtured in our industry. We recognized that and tried to create an environment and ceremonies of passage that acknowledged our staff's commitment to our startup vision. We celebrated our first 100 staff members with a welcome ceremony in which we reinforced that one day they would drive by this campus and be able to tell their grandchildren that they'd had a hand in building it for our community.

We were unstoppable. Between September 2018 and September 2020, we navigated changes and adjusted our strategy. The planning was completed, land purchased, permits obtained, persons hired, and construction commenced. We reached employee 100 in April 2022 and would add over 250 more in the next four months as we prepared to open in August 2022.

We walked toward that wish set far away. And as I cut the ribbon to open the cancer center, I reflected on that decision I'd made four years earlier. The decision to take on something new. Our whole team and I had navigated into the unknown. And together, we had found our destination.

I am most often asked, "How in the world did you open the cancer center on time and on budget during COVID?"

Let me share some takeaways that might be helpful to you on your journey.

1. Problems Can be Gifts

Many skills are transferrable, and you may know more than you think you do.

As I said, much was new to me. The closest I'd ever gotten to a construction project was picking out the furniture for my office.

I am sure the construction team was a bit worried when they saw me coming.

One of our construction managers recently shared with me that he is also getting requests from people in his industry to share our secrets for being on time. This is what he said: "Most construction project 'owner's' meetings are ceremonial and usually held monthly. They review a lot of things and focus on what has been accomplished, throw in some atta-boys, and spend little time on the problems." But then he said, "Our construction meetings were different—and so were your expectations." I still wanted to hear and celebrate the things that were going well, but those could be put in a written report and reviewed outside of the meeting. Our meetings were weekly and focused on things that threatened the timeline. This way, we could ensure resources were aligned to get the result we needed.

This was a skill learned from my years of LEAN training. This kept us focused on right outcomes and possible derailers.

2. Don't Close the Door on Crazy. Every Idea Matters …

While over the 23 months of construction there were many potential barriers to success, a few stick-out. One of those red lines that threatened the timeline was doors.

One afternoon, a new red alert showed up. All it said was "supply chain: doors." By that time, we had experienced a million different supply chain issues that we had been able to solve. I thought, "A few doors, how bad can that be?" Well, way worse than I imagined. We were not missing just a few doors; we were missing 500 doors. The lack of doors would have a trickle-down effect on other significant milestones. For example, no doors meant no sign off on a ventilation/ air flow system. What to do?

Some diligent problem solving helped us conclude that the framing and hardware could be in on time, so what about temporary doors? Yes, 500 temporary doors—and yes, it worked!

3. Work Concurrently, Not Just Consecutively.

When groups with different areas of expertise work together, I've noticed everyone tends to stay in their lane. They have a "You do your thing and I'll do mine" mentality. Project plans reinforce this. Finish one thing, then move onto the next. For example, build the doorways, then get the doors.

During our last months, we were running into several situations that required more flexibility. Moving furniture in was one of them. For those of you who usually don't have to pay attention to these types of things, there is a lot of furniture needed for 190,000 square feet of space. It takes days to move it in. Companies contracted to do this are generally scheduled well ahead. And if you miss your window, the next window is not ideal. If we could not meet our date, it would have meant a 7-10-day delay.

One day, a team member had the idea to request that the fire department allow us to move the furniture in on dates planned if we hired a 24-hour crew to hold a fire watch in the building. In our industry, regulatory agencies have tremendous influence on timelines. We submitted a formal request to the fire department to consider our situation, and they gave the go-ahead to move the furniture in. That was a close one!

4. The Goal Wasn't Just a Date—It Was Hope.

Do you know that the first Apollo mission was off target nearly 90% of the time? And that they had to keep readjusting to stay on course? And yet, history was made. Our project felt very similar. There were hundreds of examples where the project management team helped us identify problems or where the construction or cancer center teams adjusted.

Remember: Hope is a wish set far away. When we announced that we were coming to Orange County, we set hope at a particular distance: August 22, 2022. In addition to the organization that had entrusted us with resources, there was a whole community depending on us. Every day we were not open affected our patients. See, we were not just bringing a cancer center—we were bringing HOPE. And we had to honor that commitment.

We started construction on the cancer center in September 2020, in the middle of COVID-19 lockdowns, with a well-thought-out construction and licensing timeline. Target date was September 22, 2022, and exceptional performance was August 22, 2022. Of course, this team of high achievers aimed for the August date. During the project, there were legitimate logical reasons and many opportunities to push the date. So many requests, in fact, that I finally said, "Stop asking, we are sticking with 8-22-22 until midnight of 8-21-22". I knew that if we let the date slip it would never go back, and then it would be easier to keep moving it.

True to our amazing team, we all stopped asking and went full throttle. And finally, on August 22, 2022, we welcomed our first patient to the cancer center—30 days ahead of schedule.

5. The People Are EVERYTHING

We started with a team of four and grew to more than 450 in four years. No matter how well all the things mentioned above worked, no strategy or tactic can make up for having the wrong people. We were intentional about hiring the right leaders: individuals who could lead staffing plans for their respective areas and attract and hire the right people to fill their teams. We looked for experience, skills, and expertise, but just as importantly, cultural fit and a calling to this noble work. Every new hire demonstrated their ability to work amid change and ambiguity. This team was amazing and up for the challenge. Each of them did everything they could to make hope a reality.

And when I look back on this adventure, I ask myself, "Was it a good trade?"

I say Heck YES!

The rewards I received from stretching myself far outweighed the comfort and security I got from playing it safe. Although I had not done many of these things, my prior experiences provided applicable lessons that could be applied in this new situation. The motivation to do something like this, something that really mattered, came from somewhere inside, not from external rewards or affirmation.

This role has allowed me to be more personally involved in helping people find the resources they need, and it has been the most fulfilling part of my entire career.

Hope—that wish far away—was no longer a dream; it was a reality.

Today or someday, you might find yourself in the same spot I was in. How will you know it's not just a fool's errand? These are some questions to ask yourself:

- Does doing this matter? Does it have purpose and meaning?
- What does your partner say and how will it affect your family?
- Does your boss and or the board have integrity? Will they be there to support you?
- Will it make the world a better place or you a better person?
- Is it just repackaging an old story or is this truly new?
- Do you have parallels, experience, or applicable lessons that would be helpful?
- Do you have reasons to believe it is feasible, however challenging it might be?
- If you are a person of faith, have you prayed for guidance?
- Does the thought of it exhaust you because it just seems too hard?
- Will it bring you joy and keep you awake at night thinking of the possibilities?

How do you know if it's worth it? In the end, it is the preponderance of clear evidence. And for those of you who need more than just logic—the answer is in your instincts, your gut, your soul! This is the dance in between what is (the precedent—earth) and what could be (the possibilities).

So, that brings me back to that conversation with my daughter, Jessi.

No matter what you do, have the courage to try. I believe we have many opportunities presented to us in life, but most people don't have the courage to risk stepping out of their comfort zone because they fear risk, losing something, or failing. I prefer to take the position of Nelson Mandela, who said, "I never fail; I either win or learn."

> *How do you know if it's worth it? In the end, it is the preponderance of clear evidence. And for those of you who need more than just logic—the answer is in your instincts, your gut, your soul! This is the dance in between what is (the precedent—earth) and what could be (the possibilities).*

So, remember this next time you're doubting yourself, "No one's ever done it until they've done it."

And next time, let that one be you.

Annette M. Walker

Annette M. Walker is the visionary president of City of Hope Orange County. She has gained a national reputation for her industry-changing insights, outstanding leadership, and keen abilities to bring people together and achieve extraordinary results.

Twice recognized as one of the most influential leaders in U.S. healthcare by *Modern Healthcare,* Walker has been at the helm of many top organizations in her field. She considers her leadership at City of Hope among her most important roles as she is transforming cancer care for generations of patients in the nation's sixth-largest county. Walker is a featured speaker for national audiences and is the author of numerous articles on strategy, leadership, marketing, quality, planning, and management. She has received many leadership and innovation honors for her work from major institutions, organizations, and publications. A mother of six and grandmother of 13, Walker attributes her approachable leadership style to her strong family life. She is an advocate for effective work-life balance, personal growth, and development and speaks frequently on those topics. Walker holds a master's degree in healthcare administration from the University of Minnesota and a bachelor's degree in biology from Loyola Marymount University in Los Angeles.

https://www.linkedin.com/in/annette-walker/
http://www.cityofhope.org/OC
anwalker@coh.org

"*These are the stories of women who lead, who inspire, and who find their way forward, no matter the obstacles. These are the journeys of women who are quietly determined to succeed. They are optimists. They embrace the decisions that led them to where they are and accept the consequences; good or bad. They pivot. They adapt. They succeed. They ignite passion in whatever they undertake. These are the women leaders who embrace the personal and professional paths they have traveled and are grateful for those who helped them along the way. These are the stories of women who joyfully embrace the future they have designed. This read will inspire anyone who leads.*"

Joanne M. Conroy, M.D.
President and Chief Executive Officer,
Dartmouth Health

"*Reading the stories from all of the women leaders brought a large sense of connection to me, and showcases how we are all complex humans as women, leaders, sometimes mothers, partners, friends etc. Additionally, there are TOO many reminders and inspirational pieces to mention- however key takeaways from the courageous stories shared- we all have beautiful stories- we should keep this as a reminder to all we interact with, change is ok and survivable, we cannot recover time, have the courageous conversation and lead with curiosity. Reading these stories could not have come at a better time- I am navigating a current life changing decision and these stories inspired me to make the decisions I need to make!*"

Kristi Groves
Nurse Executive, Executive Director,
Veterans Health Administration,
Office of Quality Management

"*This book is uniquely inspirational and motivating. Written by amazing women who describe their hopes, dreams, experiences and yes, even some failures, in an honest, thoughtful way. This is THE book for both young and seasoned women who will delight in the shared experiences.*"

Nancy Howell Agee
Chief Executive Officer,
Carilion Clinic

"*Throughout my life, some of the biggest influences on my career in healthcare have been women: from my mother, sister, and aunts to the incredible female executives I have had the opportunity to work alongside. I've long believed in the power of sharing stories and experiences to bring us together. And this book does just that, while demonstrating courage, strength, resilience, and tenacity. Each of its contributors are trailblazers – overcoming the roadblocks they have faced in their own lives to forge a new path for the next generation of women. A rich diversity of perspectives and identities strengthens our organizations and our entire field.*"

Eugene A. Woods
Chief Executive Officer,
Advocate Health

"*Detailing the journeys of these successful women, UNSTOPPABLE will fill you with optimism and you will be empowered to take giant steps no matter how you identify, where you are in your career, or the industry in which you strive to lead. Evidenced by their creativity, character, confidence, critical thinking and entrepreneurial mindsets, these women have changed the world for so many people. We've been invited inside their heads and witnessed how they have not been taken down by tragedy, loss, or shame, rather they have grown and succeeded because of it. They openly share their vulnerability and lessons learned from failure. Envision your ongoing leadership journey and use UNSTOPPABLE as a north star!*"

Lisa Getzler
Executive Director,
Baker Institute for Entrepreneurship,
Creativity & Innovation-Lehigh University

"*As a group of highly accomplished executives with remarkable careers in the healthcare industry, these authors share their journey to success after overcoming adversity throughout their lives. During challenging moments where many would have felt defeated, their collective perseverance and optimism make you feel nothing short of inspired.*"

Brian Tierney
Chief Executive Officer,
Brian Communications

"*An essential read for any leader intent on reaching their potential on their life journey - inspiring, instructive and timely.*"

Laura S. Kaiser, FACHE
President and Chief Executive Officer,
SSM Health

"These inspirational stories show how the experiences of leaders drive their passion to make an impact. By sharing their vulnerability and authenticity, the authors have created a real-world model for aspiring leaders."

Tina Freese Decker, MHA, MSIE, FACHE
President and Chief Executive Officer,
Corewell Health

"As all great leaders know one of our top jobs is to prepare and guide the leaders of tomorrow. I am lucky enough to know many of the authors featured in UNSTOPPABLE on a personal level and they truly represent the trail blazers who are leading the way for the next generation of leaders, including my own children. UNSTOPPABLE should be required reading for all emerging leaders, men and women, in our amazing industry."

David Nash, M.D., MBA
The Dr. Raymond C and Doris N Grandon Professor of Health Policy,
Jefferson College of Population Health

"UNSTOPPABLE is a raw, honest, and penetrating account of the life experiences that have shaped these extraordinary women leaders in healthcare. Stories of their trials and triumphs form a roadmap for anyone who desires to have meaningful impact amidst personal and professional obstacles. This book is a gift to all women who seek to learn, grow, and lead."

Suja Mathew, M.D.
Chief Clinical Officer,
Atlantic Health

"UNSTOPPABLE is a collection of highly personal stories reminding us that the reality of success has no ethnicity, no race, no age, and certainly no gender. Told by some of the most reputable women in the ever-evolving healthcare industry, this book takes the reader on an emotional and inspiring journey from a refugee camp and an abusive relationship to impactful C-suite careers in companies and boardrooms. While each chapter is flooded with hard-won wisdom, what's most impressive is the unique marriage of humility and pride in which each story is told. If you are ready to rise above adversity and are seeking motivation to win life's defining moments, then put this book on your required reading list."

Sam Davidson
Chief Operating Officer,
Geocann

"UNSTOPPABLE is a captivating collection that celebrates the unwavering spirit of women. From the heart-wrenching experiences of loss to the unwavering determination to create a better future, these stories remind us of the profound strength and compassion that lie within us all."

Shivani Rajput
Principal, Administration,
Northwell Health

"This appropriately titled book chronicles both the trials and tribulations of some of the country's most dynamic and driven female executives. The common themes of courage, resilience, and tenacity found in these women should inspire an entire generation of females to rise above the ancient patriarchal noise that stifled women for centuries. The fact that most of these women in the health industry are innate healers of the human condition should not be lost on the reader. Kudos to the trailblazers, male and female, who believed in the early potential of this group of esteemed leaders. As Sue MacInnes suggests, "whatever was sent my way would be something I'd have to figure out and rise above." Not only have these women risen above their personal and professional challenges but they have proved that great success begins with great compassion."

Scott Tinley, Ph.D.
2X Ironman World Champion

"A great read for anyone looking for stories of inspiration, courage, and lessons in life that can immediately be put to use. Reminded me of the classic Dale Carnegie book, How to Stop Worrying and Start Living, that's a book I've reread many times and no doubt I'll do the same with UNSTOPPABLE!"

Andy Mills
President, Medline

"This book is a must-read for anyone looking to pursue their passions! I am so impressed by these fearless leaders, all from diverse and fascinating backgrounds. The resilience, determination, and success throughout these women's lives are a powerful reminder that believing in yourself and leading with love will always persevere. UNSTOPPABLE offers inspiring lessons for all ages, especially during periods of transformation."

Deborah Adler
Healthcare Design and Innovation Leader,
Adler Design

"*Becoming a leader in healthcare requires a person to apply the knowledge, skills, and life experiences that have shaped who they are and to take advantage of the opportunities they are presented. UNSTOPPABLE provides the compelling stories of a remarkable group of women who did persevere and achieved amazing careers as leaders in healthcare. Each story highlights some of the adversities faced and how these women took control of their own destinies as they developed their vision of what success should be. While UNSTOPPABLE was written with a goal of encouraging other women to achieve their success, I learned a lot of important lessons while reading the stories. I believe many of the lessons could apply to all of us who strive for success in our careers.*"

Dale W. Bratzler, DO, MPH
Dean, Hudson College of Public Health

"*These beautiful stories of courage, strength and love remind us of the importance of sharing, nurturing and inspiring each other.*"

Amy Perry
President & Chief Operating Officer,
Banner Health

"*Our personal stories have the power to change how we see ourselves and each other. UNSTOPPABLE offers inspiration to all of us as we look to navigate our career and, more importantly, our lives, with authenticity, purpose, and power.*"

Renee DeSilva
Chief Executive Officer,
The Health Management Academy

"*The stories in this book are amazing, and they are accessible to anyone trying to get their arms around this journey called life. "Put a Woman in Charge" and they will be UNSTOPPABLE!*"

Thomas Liebman
Chairman, Coilcraft

Printed in the USA
CPSIA information can be obtained
at www.ICGtesting.com
BVHW031538220823
668780BV00003BA/23

9 781961 781177